D1288686

ROUNDING THE TURN

Michael Francis Quinn (1856–1932), founder.

$15.00

ROUNDING THE TURN

. . . .

1906-1956

Compiled by MARION KELLEY

QUINN & BODEN COMPANY, INC.
Rahway *New Jersey*

Printed in the United States of America
Library of Congress Catalog Card Number: 56–13481

To the Memory of

MICHAEL FRANCIS QUINN

and

JOHN J. QUINN

CONTENTS

Contents

FOREWORD

The story of a book manufacturing plant is essentially a part of a larger whole—the cultural and economic history of a nation and an age. Without books there would never have been an American way of life. By books we educate our children. In books we store our knowledge. Through books we communicate with each other. From books we recapture our past and project our future. Out of books come the faiths and the ideals by which we are sustained. For a civilization such as ours there can be no end to the making of books.

After fifty years we at Quinn and Boden still feel, as each new title is delivered to its publisher, something of the same pride and satisfaction with which we completed our first one. There is a piece of our own knowledge and experience and craftsmanship built into each title and each volume. We know that the books we make will, some of them, go to the ends of the earth, and that others will become part of their owner's most cherished and individual of all possessions, the personal library.

Foreword

This brief history of Quinn and Boden reflects, we hope, the sense of pride with which we all look back on our first fifty years. If it also conveys to our friends some portion of the sense of pleasure we have felt in working with and for them, we shall be grateful. And a part of pleasure is the sense of anticipation. We look forward with eagerness to the books of the next fifty years and the friends for whom we shall be making them.

JAMES T. QUINN

September 20, 1956

ROUNDING THE TURN

• • • • • • • •

A SHORT STOP IN RAHWAY

• • • • • • • •

On the station platform, as the smoke of the departing train drifted away, the lone arrival from New York paused for his first full view of the town he planned to visit so briefly. He lingered no longer than was necessary. It was midafternoon on this August day of 1906, and the blistering heat of the summer sun urged him on to a cooler and more sheltered spot.

Under other circumstances, Michael Francis Quinn might have been prompted to take a longer and more searching look. The town before him was Rahway and the single business call he was about to make there had in it the elements of destiny's handiwork. For Mr. Quinn's short stop in Rahway was to lengthen to a lifetime in the course of which he and this small New Jersey city would have a profound effect each upon the other.

At the moment, however, he had little time to waste. Once he had solicited an advertisement here for the trade paper he published in the metropolis, he intended to return to his office, train schedules permitting. He was half ready to regret stopping at all, for only curiosity had brought him.

A big wooden sign, billboard-fashion, was responsible. Spread-eagled atop a building not far from the tracks, it caught his attention whenever he rode by on his way from New York to Philadelphia. "The Mershon Company, Printers," it read. Today he hoped to make the Mershon Company a customer.

As he strode briskly toward the business district, his keen eyes appraised the rolling meadows around Rahway, by then turning a little brown in the midsummer dry spell. They took in the neat shops lining both sides of the main street; the horse-drawn drays, farm carts and occasional buggies that jostled each other for smooth going through the powdery dust of the unpaved road; the pedestrians pursuing their errands along tarred sidewalks, behind a sparse hedge of hitching posts. Rahway, even in the oppressive midsummer heat, had a lively look about it, and Michael Quinn liked what he saw.

That he did so was fortunate—both for Rahway and for himself. It sustained his interest in the town despite a discouraging next few minutes. The Mershon firm, he learned in a talk with William Mershon, its head, was not interested in placing an ad. In fact they had just decided to sell out the business they had founded a quarter century before as lads out of school.

At this turn in the conversation, Mr. Quinn set aside both his sales talk and any disappointment he may have felt. He devoted the next few moments to a bit of rapid mental arithmetic. Those moments, to all intents and purposes, witnessed the creation of the printing firm of Quinn & Boden, Inc., now celebrating the fiftieth year of its existence.

Here, Michael Quinn recognized, was his opportunity to realize the dream held close to his heart since boyhood—that of operating a print shop of his own. Printer's ink had been in his veins since he first went to work at fifteen for the Ira Bradley bookbinding firm in Boston.

Since leaving Bradley's in 1892, he had engaged in several business ventures, all of them successful to a degree. But none had given him quite the satisfaction which he felt, almost instinctively, that the printing business could. The question was how to open the door to opportunity's knocking.

Characteristically, having assessed the possibilities and found them good, having faced up to the risks and found them not insurmountable, Michael Quinn acted.

It was early evening when he and William Mershon walked out of the plant, the latter convinced that he and his brothers at last could retire, Michael Quinn carefully tucking an option on the business in his inner pocket for safekeeping.

As he stood on the platform a few minutes later awaiting the Manhattan-bound train, he looked back over the town where he was to spend a most enjoyable quarter of a century. Above the trees, motionless in the calm of the summer evening, a pale new moon was delicately etched in the deepening blue haze of the August sky.

To one superstitiously or even romantically inclined this might have suggested a happy portent for his new beginnings. But Michael Quinn was a practical man with no time for moon-gazing. His thoughts were concerned with various means of raising a very substantial amount of money in a very short time.

Back in New York that night, he called an old friend, Benjamin Boden, then foreman of the bindery at the printing and publishing house of P. F. Collier. The following day over the luncheon table they decided to join forces in the new venture.

Between them, they were able to raise the sum of $10,000. The Rahway National Bank, taking into account the integrity of the new owners, the value of the plant and its business possibilities under the new management, advanced the balance. The principal was to be paid off in monthly installments over a period of years.

On October 1, 1906, undaunted by debt and the growing financial uneasiness which was to erupt in the 1907 panic, the infant printing firm of Quinn & Boden went officially into business.

Sharing responsibilities was John J. Quinn, the twenty-five-year-old son of the owner, who as a graduate accountant came to work in his father's office. A few months later John A. Buckley, who had worked with Benjamin Boden at P. F. Collier in New York, joined the staff as plant manager.

A New York office was opened at 41 Union Square as

a convenient contact point for publishers. Joseph Struthers was installed here to head its sales force.

The partners had no way of knowing, during those early days of financing and refinancing, that in a few short years they were to number on their roster of authors some of the most illustrious names in letters; that their presses would be kept busy turning out thousands of Navy manuals on government contracts during World War I; that they were to become one of the largest printing houses in the country specializing in textbooks. Yet all these things were accomplished by Quinn & Boden long in advance of their reaching the half-century post.

Company buildings in 1906 consisted of a three-story brick structure facing Jackson Avenue, with an ell-shaped building jutting along Broad Street to join it at right angles. Over-all floor space was approximately 40,000 square feet.

The equipment varied. There were ten presses of diverse makes. An original Gordon press, manufactured in Rahway, was installed first by the elder Mershon on the third floor of his home on Milton Avenue in 1877 to foster a hobby for his sons. When the hobby showed signs of becoming big business, it was moved to a separate building and became the nucleus of the printing plant. Today it stands inside the door at the entrance to the office—a sort of testimonial to progress.

A notation of its purchase on the books of the old Mershon Company, now in the Quinn & Boden vaults, lists in a fine Spencerian hand, "Pa bought the Press for $38."

Also a part of the heterogeneous plant appointments were a folding machine of 1880 vintage and a Smythe sewing machine. It was with these tools that Quinn & Boden began printing approximately 4,000 books a day in 1906 with the aid of some seventy-five workers in all departments. Skilled personnel as we know them today were only in the top echelon of workers.

The first few years were the kind that tested courage. In 1907, during the Theodore Roosevelt administration, came a panic that forced some of the largest and most reputable publishing houses in New York to meet their obligations with I O Us. All were of unqualified integrity, but they felt the pinch. As for Quinn & Boden, there was the not-too-simple matter of meeting payrolls each week, which kept the principals awake nights trying to figure ways and means. On more than one occasion it is recorded that the wallets of the executives were much slimmer than those of the workers when the plant paid off on Saturday.

A large publishing house in New York failed, owing the firm about $20,000. At times like this, it fell to Mr. Quinn's lot to call on such customers as Mr. Bristol of Henry Holt and Co., Mr. Grosset of Grosset & Dunlap, and Mr. Dodd of Dodd, Mead & Co. to ask for an advance on bills not yet due in order to meet the payrolls.

Like Rome, the present firm was not built in a day, or even in the first few years. Difficulties at the start were varied and many. The name of Quinn & Boden had been placed on the building less than a month when the company encountered its first setback—one that was close to catastrophic. A huge wooden water tank on the roof of the main building collapsed, sending a cascade of tons of water through the structure and causing several thousand dollars' worth of damage.

Ruefully surveying the soggy wreckage, the owners still congratulated themselves on one thing: the accident had happened late on a Saturday afternoon. There was no one in the building to get hurt.

But these were the setbacks that put the spurs to courage and ingenuity. New business came in 1910. World events were making news; modern inventions occupied the headlines and Quinn & Boden shared in the revival of national prosperity.

Across the ocean an airplane successfully spanned the English Channel; the North and South Poles were being explored. In 1911 a winged machine flew across our continent. It was the dawn of a new era, with promise of great changes in all lines of business and ways of life.

History, as usual, had a way of overlapping. Only a few blocks from the plant, horses were still stepping briskly along the old stagecoach route, once an Indian trail which was to become the Lincoln Highway, but the spirited animals were shying less violently at the honking horns and loud exhausts of the automobiles which rattled by at speeds of from fifteen to twenty miles an hour.

It was during the first decade of the firm's life, in 1914,

that the traders of the world turned speculative eyes toward Panama, where completion of the canal opened a vista of shortened commercial routes and established America as a dominant power on the seas as well as on land.

The magic effects of this development, however, were a long time in making themselves felt at home. They set off the first fitful stirrings of a new prosperity, but the Rahway plant, as a young company, was content to settle for a modest nine per cent increase in gross sales in the six-year period beginning in 1910.

Then in August, 1914, came the revolver shot that terminated the life of Archduke Ferdinand of Austria-Hungary and touched off the war that was to engulf the world. In that conflict the United States remained neutral until the sinking of the liner *Lusitania* by a German submarine in 1917, with the loss of many American lives. On April 6 of that year, Congress declared war on Germany, and the European debacle became the First World War.

Bands began to play "It's a Long, Long Way to Tipperary" and "Over There." As did other Rahway business houses, Quinn & Boden translated patriotic fervor into practical action. On a memorable Saturday afternoon when executives and plant personnel had gathered for an outdoor flag raising, Michael Quinn gave his men this solemn pledge:

"Any employee who answers his country's call to fight against Germany need not fear for his dependents.

This firm will see that none come to want during his absence."

Since the country was not then equipped with sufficient camps to train rookie soldiers, Michael Quinn offered to provide a drill-master for his own men. On the distaff side, first-aid classes were organized in the plant by the Red Cross.

Lights at Quinn & Boden's burned through the night during the exciting war times. "The Blue Jacket's Manual," required reading for every man in the U.S. naval forces, was being turned out at the rate of ten to twelve thousand copies a week. War books, too, were hurried through the presses.

In May 1917, a month after the United States had entered the war, "Over the Top," a 500,000-copy best-seller by Arthur Guy Empey, streamed from their presses to put a new phrase into the language.

A native of Ogden, Utah, Empey went to France as a volunteer with the British Army, and was invalided home as a result of wounds received in the battle of the Somme. Writing eloquently of the first war American boys ever had fought on European soil, he captured the public imagination with his tough and vivid narrative style.

The men who followed him into battle from the Quinn & Boden organization were, for the most part, volunteers. By some grim twist of fate, the very first man to go was the only casualty suffered by the Rahway printing contingent. He was young Jack Mulvey, who died in action with one of the first American units to reach France, and whose name today lives on in that of the Mulvey-Ditmars Post 681 of the Veterans of Foreign Wars in Rahway. Other recruits from the company's ranks went through the conflict unscathed, save for minor wounds.

On the home front, meanwhile, company officials had to cope with manpower shortages, heatless Mondays, and once with a complete lack of fuel that forced the plant to shut down for a two-week period. Thus it was with a sigh of relief that they tied down the whistle on top of the plant that November morning in 1918, to join other Rahway factories in shrieking the welcome news that the "war to end war" at last was over.

But it seemed an interminable time before trained personnel were free to return from service. Jim Lints, who now has a 45-year record with the firm, recalls how, after the Armistice, John Quinn appealed for his release directly to the Adjutant General. The war had ended before Jim had a chance to get into battle, but there was a lively skirmish going on at the plant, where they were trying to print thousands of copies of the Carnegie "Endowment for International Peace" with a skeleton staff. Jim remembers being mustered out early in January. He relates, too, how they worked around the clock to turn out the increasing number of new orders that poured in after the war.

By February, still others of the boys began to trickle back from Army camps in this country. The scenes and conditions to which they returned were a far cry, in some respects, from what they had left in 1917. Prohibition was just around the corner. Women were campaigning for the vote and were invading business houses and industrial plants on every side. Quinn & Boden was no exception. More and more women swung into the firm's working ranks. Some of them are there today.

In the head office, the postwar era found a strong executive group directing the fortunes of the company. Michael Quinn, succeeding to the presidency after the brief illness and untimely death of Benjamin Boden in 1913, had purchased his late partner's interests, but continued operations under the original firm name.

A man of fifty when he entered upon the venture which was to become his life's work, Michael Quinn was well equipped by temperament, training, and experience to pilot the young company through its first trying years. The hardships he had overcome in his youth might well have served as material for one of Horatio Alger's classics.

He was the youngest in a family of nine children and spent his boyhood in the little lumber and farming community of Woodstock, New Brunswick, Canada. Living conditions were rough and primitive. The only water in the Quinn home came in buckets hauled up by a windlass from a well at the back door. Candles furnished the only lighting.

In the homes of their well-to-do neighbors, there were oil lamps, but regardless of wealth, every house in Woodstock was heated by wood stoves. Michael Quinn recalled that he was quite a sizable lad before he saw his first chunk of coal. There were no public schools, and the only way a child could learn his ABC's was to attend a small private school conducted by a local schoolmaster.

Even then, schooling was limited to a few weeks each year—in the spring and fall. Weather conditions in winter were too severe, and in summer every member of the family was needed to work on the farm. There was little money in circulation; business was carried on largely through barter.

This was the environment in which Mr. Quinn spent the first years of his life. His older brothers left one by one to go to the United States, where they enlisted in the Union Army and fought during the Civil War. When Mike Quinn was only fifteen years of age, his father was killed in a railroad accident, and the boy went down to Boston to seek a way to earn his living.

On his first job, in the Ira Bradley book bindery on Washington Street near Adams Square, he worked from 7 A.M. to 6 P.M., Saturdays included. After work he walked back to his rooming house in the South End of Boston, washed, changed his clothes, ate supper, and then walked over to the West End, where he attended night school. He continued this stint for seven years; the education he thus secured carried him through life.

Mr. Quinn learned his trade step by step, first as an apprentice, then as journeyman, assistant foreman, and finally as superintendent of the bindery. He also became active in the Knights of Labor, which a few years later developed into the American Federation of Labor.

A Short Stop in Rahway

When his own company was functioning smoothly in 1915 Michael Quinn found time to enter into the civic life of Rahway. Joining forces with one of the town's leading citizens, the late Edward S. Savage, he sponsored a project to dredge the Rahway River so that it would be navigable, as it had been in early Colonial times. Serving as members of the League of New Jersey Waterways Association, these two civic-minded businessmen worked tirelessly but without success to interest the authorities in the undertaking.

Practically everything that concerned the general welfare and advancement of Rahway held Michael Quinn's interest. When he first purchased the plant there had been flippant remarks from a few of his well-meaning friends: "You never will be satisfied over there; it is too far from the big city"—"The town is just a whistle stop"—"No background"—were a few of the inciting barbs. Someone jestingly made him a bet, "You never will find a house in Rahway where George Washington spent the night."

Oddly enough, Michael Quinn had owned the company less than six months when he learned that an old house across from his plant, since torn down to provide space for an employees' tennis court, had been historically labeled as a site where the General had rested overnight.

By delving further into history books, some being printed in his own plant, Mr. Quinn learned that Rahway had been a town of some consequence during the American Revolution. It seemed doubtful that General

Washington had time to pause anywhere, even for an evening, with the British so close on his heels during that winter of 1776–77.

It is historically authenticated, however, that the army's commissary department was dispatched to Rahway out of reach of the enemy during Washington's strategic retreat across New Jersey into Pennsylvania. All barns in the town and outlying districts were filled to capacity with the stores and ammunition of our Revolutionary forces. It also is recorded that the British did not eat in Rahway that winter.

The town's bid for historical fame came early. The Lincoln Highway, that now runs parallel to the Quinn & Boden plant, was the old stagecoach route between New York and Philadelphia. Rahway was the first overnight stop. The old Peace Tavern on St. George's Avenue was the spot where the weary travelers stopped to dine, rest the horses, and chat around blazing fireplaces before retiring to canopied four-posters. It is now, quite fittingly, the Girl Scout Headquarters.

In the early 1800's the town had 350 to 400 houses and a population of some 3,000 people. There were stores of various kinds, twenty-five taverns, three public buildings, and five churches of different denominations.

That education was as much a matter of pride with the early Rahway settlers as it is with the townsfolk today, is recorded in their special mention of the "Athenian" academy which accommodated 150 scholars, "with a lecture room on the first floor where the important educational subjects were discussed to aid pupils in the general knowledge of the arts and sciences."

A historical notation also revealed something of a gem in the social annals of Rahway's early history. On August 24, 1824, leaders among the townspeople arranged a ball at the old Peace Tavern for Marquis de Lafayette, who was en route by stagecoach from New York to Philadelphia. The occasion was a visit at the invitation of the U.S. Congress, almost half a century after the gallant Frenchman had seen the birth of the nation to which he contributed so freely of his wealth and influence.

The story is told that more than one stagecoach came in from Manhattan that day bringing celebrities for the brilliant party. And the town was in festive mood. Gay banners decorated the inn and special dishes in the French tradition were prepared for the big dinner. As lovely ladies in crinolines and light silks fanned themselves on the wide veranda, long since removed to extend the highway, the Marquis, unmindful of the August heat, lavished compliments, not only on the ladies but about the improvements of their town in the past four decades.

At that time, 1824, Rahway was manufacturing for export such commodities as shoes, hats, boats, carriages, cabinet furniture, ready-made clothing, soap, candles, cotton and woolen goods, coach lace, carriages and snuff, along with plated wear for harnesses and carriages. The capital required for such manufacture and goods was listed at about $300,000, and the value of the exports at approximately $1,200,000.

By 1906, when Quinn & Boden moved in, the town's population had grown to between nine and ten thousand people. Merck and Company had been established seven years and was housed in one small plant. The Three-in-One Oil Company was a small factory which later was taken over by the Dr. Lyons Tooth Powder Company. The Regina Company was manufacturing music boxes. Today they are in the more lucrative business of vacuum cleaners and floor polishers.

With the gradual wane of the barrel business, the Hamilton Cooperage works closed their small plant soon after World War I, but the more enterprising Graves Carriage factory diverted their output in 1918 to automobile bodies. The Wheatena Company arrived in 1912 and is still doing a thriving business.

Meanwhile Quinn & Boden was concentrating its energies on the strenuous business of growing up. Developing with it was young John Quinn, a quiet lad with a flair for administration. His personal tragedy was an unfortunate accident which occurred while he was a cadet on the S.S. *Enterprise.* This resulted in the loss of his right hand and terminated his dream of a career at sea.

Years later there was found tucked away among old papers in his father's desk a letter from Rear Admiral Robert E. Coontz, then Commander of the S.S. *Enterprise,* citing the bravery of eighteen-year-old John during a terrific storm at sea. The State of Massachusetts gave him $2,500 compensation which the young chap judiciously applied to his education and the recharting of his career.

While John's disability barred him from the mechanical departments of the plant, it sharpened his ambition to master administrative details.

The firm burst out of the initial confines of the old Mershon plant in the early 1920's. By then it was found necessary to build a new two-story building adjoining the railroad as an addition to the upper and lower binderies. This unit was completed in 1924, and was followed shortly by a new warehouse, erected across the street from the main building, to house bound stock and other material ready for shipment.

That the leaders of the enterprise were hardly being rash in authorizing this much expansion was evident from the record. Between 1916 and 1921 its gross sales had risen by ninety-three per cent, and the period between 1921 and 1926 was to witness another thirty-five per cent increase on top of that. Quinn & Boden, even to the eye of the most cautious of prognosticators, appeared to be in business to stay.

YEARS OF SOLID GROWTH

• • • • • • • •

A quiet man named Calvin Coolidge was in the White House, another one named Lindbergh had soloed across the Atlantic a few months earlier, and Admiral Byrd was being hailed as a national hero upon his return from the Antarctic when Quinn & Boden came of age in 1927.

It was a pleasant time in which to achieve one's majority. Prosperity was definitely here to stay. The land everywhere was one of smiling promise—and for the printing firm in Rahway some of the promises already were coming true.

In its first twenty-one years, the company had expanded production from 4,000 books printed daily in 1906 to 15,000 a day. Additional building had provided 175,000 square feet of floor space, and the firm had acquired many of those open fields around the plant that so attracted Michael Quinn on his first visit. If needful, a plant twice the size of the 1927 establishment could be erected on the ground available.

During this era new equipment, which included the latest types of modern printing and binding machinery, had been added at a cost of more than half a million dollars.

Electricity for lighting purposes and power for mechanical operations, formerly generated in the plant, was now supplied by the Public Service Corporation. But a six months' reserve of fuel was kept on hand at all times to forestall emergencies, along with a well-staffed machine shop to keep equipment in good running order.

Transportation facilities had been excellent from the start. A private siding connected with the main line of the Pennsylvania Railroad; the Lincoln Highway was a few blocks away. Now the firm had acquired large trucks to ship the bulk of their output, and well-paved highways meant increased speed for deliveries.

Michael Quinn was pleased with the speeding-up process. He had often said, "One thing which the large-edition binder is able to offer the publisher is speed in production, and that tempo must be carried on through delivery. Publishers often face a situation where speed in the production of a book is almost as essential as 'fast freight' for perishable foodstuffs."

He regarded the profitable book as a "perishable" commodity; his bindery was equipped with the best modern quantity-production machinery to speed the printed word to the market.

Mr. Quinn's feeling about this is exemplified by a time back in January, 1920, remembered by many at Quinn

& Boden, when the then young firm of Alfred Harcourt and Donald Brace, just trying to get a foothold in the publishing business as Harcourt, Brace & Co., were anxiously awaiting a shipment of John Maynard Keynes' "The Economic Consequences of the Peace."

Not expecting it to become a best-seller, Mr. Harcourt had ordered a first edition from Quinn & Boden of 4,000 copies. But glowing front-page reviews all over the country soon depleted the stock in bookstores and the young publishers sent a frantic S O S to Rahway. Of this incident Alfred Harcourt tells the story in a personal account of his early years in printing, published in 1951.

"New York was having one of its record snowstorms, and the streets were so blocked with drifts that the truck from Quinn & Boden, who had printed the book, couldn't make deliveries, but they sent man after man by train from their plant in Rahway, New Jersey, with as many copies as each could carry. The first edition was wiped out; we knew what harm it would do to the sale if the book went out of stock just when public demand was riding high. We had unfilled orders for 9,000 copies. Lincoln's Birthday was coming, which gave a three-day week end. Mr. Quinn, a grand old Irishman, had promised this as a holiday to his men, but he went to them and explained that this was the great chance for those two young men, Don and me, to make good. A carload of paper for it had just arrived. So that plant stayed open night and day for those three days, and we got 22,000 bound books the next Tuesday."

By 1927 a comparatively small number of publishers were paying Quinn & Boden over a million dollars a year for producing their books. The policy of housing the entire manufacturing process under one roof, the high standard of quality production and easy accessibility to the metropolitan market, was paying off in dollars.

It was still the rollicking twenties and no one thought in terms of depression. But the panic of 1907 had left its mark on Michael Quinn. Through the ensuing years he insisted on building a sound financial backlog for unforeseen emergencies.

When the crash came in October, 1929, and black depression settled over the country, it was Quinn & Boden's turn to extend credit to their publishing houses, thereby cementing lifelong business and personal friendships, as well as leveling off somewhat the score of old kindnesses extended.

John J. Quinn's flair for figures and his system of keeping close watch on costs were now to prove their real worth. It had not been easy in the beginning for the junior partner to sell his ideas to the founders who had learned their trade from the business side of the machines. But they finally were to realize that a cost-accounting system was the true compass which indicated at a glance whether business was heading for a safe port or the shoals.

Cost accounts were not too well known or generally applied to business in the early days. The imposition of Federal income taxes after World War I forced many plants to install the system. Tax examiners insisted on seeing the evidence and asked that figures rather than glib talk tell the story.

John Quinn's staunch belief in the cost-accounting system led to frequent discussions with his father. Business, however, was moving along at a good clip and the elder Mr. Quinn did not take the problem too seriously. Nevertheless, the suggestions of his son were not completely discounted by the father. Factors were coming into play which led him to realize that young John's ideas had merit.

For example, the plant had now grown to physical proportions that required competent organization and up-to-date methods if it were to function efficiently and at top capacity. Volume of business too, with its gratifying record of annual increase, called for a new modernized financial structure to cope with its complexities.

Michael Quinn first sought the counsel of his good friend Alfred Harcourt to whose firm of Harcourt, Brace and Co. he had been among the first to extend credit when they opened for business.

The outcome of their discussion was that Quinn & Boden retained William C. Heaton & Co., certified public accountants, who instituted the necessary measures to reorganize the firm as a corporation.

All preferred stock was retained by Michael Quinn; the common stock and control of the business passed from his hands to be shared equally by his sons and by John A. Buckley, secretary and plant manager, who had entered the business in 1907.

Years of Solid Growth

When complete reorganization was effected in 1925, John Quinn's "theories" became the basic principles of the concern which operates today as Quinn & Boden Company, Incorporated. Financial guesswork was eliminated and the easy-going, old-fashioned methods of reckoning costs and profits were replaced by the new economic yardsticks which provided exact figures for operational costs and overhead.

The advantages of the cost-accounting system which John Quinn had advocated, served him well as heavier responsibilities were placed upon his shoulders. Failing health had already reduced his father's working day to a few hours, and through the years of the latter's decline, John Quinn was forced to assume the full burden of the business.

When in April, 1932, death claimed Michael Quinn in his seventy-sixth year, the founder left his twenty-six-year-old business in sound condition, with an experienced and competent successor to chart its course. Today, in the Cue-Bee Club built for his employees, and which he did not live to see completed, there is a modest memorial plaque honoring Michael Quinn and his achievements.

When they dedicated this, his associates paid eloquent and affectionate tribute to Michael Quinn the man. "He was," in their words, "a typical American businessman. He worked hard, year after year, for long hours, and made many sacrifices before he finally reached the goal of success. Always unassuming and unpretentious, considerate of the rights of others, generous with his time and means, ever ready to extend a helping hand to those in need, he was a credit to his country, state, and the city of Rahway. He was an ideal American, loving husband and father—and we looked upon him as a friend and confidant, rather than as an employer." Rarely has a man been paid a more affectionate tribute—or one more deserved.

John Quinn immediately assumed the post of president, an office he was to fill until he became Chairman of the Board of Directors fourteen years later. Named Treasurer at this time was John Quinn's younger brother James, who with five years of practical working experience in different departments was equipped for an executive job. He became familiar with plant operations during his school days, when summer vacations were spent learning the business shoulder to shoulder with the people in each department. It was not until 1927, after he had been graduated from Notre Dame University, that James Quinn entered the workers' ranks at the plant on a full-time basis.

Young Quinn's entry into the business coincided with the "boom and bust" era that sent American business into a long, disheartening skid. Orders eased off and the firm tightened its belt, economically speaking, but kept its working force intact. There were no dreaded dismissal slips in the pay envelopes at the Rahway, New Jersey, plant.

Those who followed Michael Quinn had reason to be thankful for his wise thrift in hoarding strong financial reserves for the "rainy day." The deluge had come, and in

1933 the fortunes of the firm touched their lowest point in a decade. Then dawned the blackest day of all, when President Franklin Roosevelt's edict of a bank holiday brought the vast machinery of industrial America to a grinding halt.

Now it was John Quinn who met the emergency. From the firm's vault there was forthcoming a special cash reserve sufficient for the payroll and for immediate operating expenses. There was no need to close the doors; the plant could stay in business until the banks reopened.

During the next few years, the firm in Rahway struggled on, extending a helping hand where it could, but compelled to watch grimly as other business houses foundered in the economic storm. Those were the years of bread lines—but Quinn & Boden did not add its employees to them.

The United States went off the gold standard, set up the PWA to relieve immediate distress among the jobless, and laid the foundations of a Social Security system to help make sure the same disaster would never strike again—or at least not with the same devastating force.

But even as these things were occupying the attention of America at home, the stage was being set abroad for a greater tragedy still, one which was to engulf many a Quinn & Boden official and employee in the years immediately ahead.

A fanatic Hitler gained control in Germany, seized the Rhineland, bullied and then took over Czechoslovakia and Austria. Italy and Japan embarked on careers of conquest in their chosen spheres, and the dictator nations sharpened their weapons in Spain's civil war.

Meantime, America had rounded the corner economically. Desperate measures taken in Washington helped the nation lift itself by its bootstraps, and slowly the black cloud of depression lifted. The printing house in Rahway, due to conservative management and aggressive selling, was among the first to feel the balmy breeze of renewed business activity.

By 1937 the need for a larger storage warehouse was imperative; two years later another was erected. This latter building had been completed when news of the German invasion of Poland was broadcast. If war came again, could America remain neutral?

Treachery was rampant across the sea. Italy's dagger was turned against her neighbor France; England, ill-equipped for war, fought alone as Germany loosed a rain of bombs upon her islands.

As history wrote the grim and terrible chronicle, men took to their pens. Printing was experiencing another spurt in output. Pressed for storage space, the firm rushed a new warehouse to completion in the fall of 1941. A few months later came the sneak attack on Pearl Harbor by the Japanese. America was again at war.

A new brand of books began to roll off the presses—Ford's "What the Citizen Should Know About the Army"; Baldwin's "What the Citizen Should Know About the Navy"; Powell's "What the Citizen Should Know About the Coast Guard."

There were new editions of "The Army Officer's Guide" and "The Naval Officer's Guide." Manuscripts on war subjects were hurried into type—Floherty's "Aviation from Shop to Sky"; MacLeish's "Aircraft Spotter," and Bollinger's "Financing Defense Orders," to name just a few.

The "blitzkrieg" and a new type of warfare channeled the Quinn & Boden output into technological and science fields; there was growing demand for such books, which the firm met while retaining their old accounts for popular novels.

There was no difficulty in obtaining orders; the problem was how to turn them out. This new brand of war called every available man into service. Personnel in all departments was cut.

In normal times the work load would have required a force of 500 workers for day and night shifts. But manpower shortage had stripped the plant down to 385 men and women. They worked heroically, turning night into day with a schedule that went around the clock.

A group of women, former employees, some of whom had been retired but were familiar with the work, offered their services. They reported at 5:30 P.M. and worked until midnight inspecting and wrapping books. The plant had a fleet of station wagons to call for and return them to their homes each night. Soon this loyal band of energetic troupers became known as "The Rocking Chair Crew" and as such they have an honored place in the firm's annals.

The government, meanwhile, was importuned for exemption of skilled workmen in printing and allied arts. It was argued that the same exemptions were required here as in war production industries, since the output was vital to the war effort.

But Washington was not convinced by the fact that six to eight years were required to learn the varied techniques for making books and that it was not possible to hire 4-F's to fill in these gaps.

As proof, Quinn & Boden printed a volume listing some 1,300 current titles, virtually all of a technical nature. Under Group A were 556 titles from nineteen different publishers for use in school training courses, colleges, naval training centers, service academies, industrial plants producing war materials, hospitals, and Army camps.

These included volumes on Aeronautics, Communications, Engineering, Radio and Television, Military Science, Seamanship, Sea Lanes in Wartime, Map Reading and Avigation. Under a heading of "general reading" were White's "They Were Expendable," "People Under Hitler," by Deuel, Schevill's "History of Europe," "How America Lives," by Furnas, Ayling's "R.A.F.," Johnston's "Flying Fleets" and "Flying Squadrons" and Chambrun's "I Saw France Fall."

For elementary and junior high school needs were works on Organic Chemistry, Farm Soil Fundamentals, Animal Husbandry, Fundamentals of Civil and Structural Engineering, Mathematics, Home Economics, Physics, Astronomy, Geology, Electronics, Psychology and some twenty different textbooks for nurses' training courses.

An impressive list of 744 books was catalogued under Group B, for special use in high schools, colleges, and universities throughout the country. These comprised foreign language textbooks, as well as books on Metallurgy, Calculus, Surveying, Astronomy and Navigation, Biological Sciences, Forestry, Industrial Processes, Mineralogy, Political Science, Law, and Medicine.

While it constituted a source of quiet pride to the Quinn & Boden staff in demonstrating the significance and tremendous variety of their output, this concise volume of forty-five pages, well catalogued and very much to the point though it was, failed in its mission. Washington regretted that such necessary production should be impaired, but every able-bodied man was needed either at the front or in direct war production. While the book undoubtedly helped to keep personnel on the job, it brought no replacements for those already in the service.

Thus Quinn & Boden entered the crucial phase of the great conflict facing serious problems, but determined to contribute its full share to the winning of final victory.

CHANGE AND CHALLENGE

• • • • • • • •

The early days of 1942 were grim ones for the nation. The headlines screamed of the loss of Corregidor, the death march on Bataan, the enemy push southward to Guadalcanal. New words were being introduced to the American vocabulary. On the home front, the talk was of victory gardens, rationing, and quislings; of Jimmy Doolittle and "Shangri-La."

In Rahway, Quinn & Boden suffered other setbacks at that time in addition to the exigencies of war. The country had been involved in the conflict only a few months when the company lost another of its veteran top executives with the passing of John A. Buckley.

Still another loss, although a temporary one, was the departure of James T. Quinn, then the firm's treasurer, to offer his services to his country. In September of 1942 he reported to the Armed Guard Officers' Training Center, and three months later was assigned to the tanker S.S. *Gulf Gem*.

Mr. Quinn made many perilous crossings of the Atlantic in the year that followed before he was called to Washington, D.C., for service in the Distribution Division of the Navy's Bureau of Personnel. He remained on this duty until the war was nearly over and the Bureau returned to peacetime activities.

Problems posed by the Second World War for Quinn & Boden were sharpened and intensified far beyond those of World War I. The draft had depleted the staff to the point where only a skeleton crew remained. This tiny force worked feverishly to manufacture the increasing number of textbooks written to cover the new fields and problems of modern warfare.

Various wartime restrictions further complicated matters, among them the absolute ban on all building not considered essential to the war effort. As a result even the company's newest warehouse, covering some 30,000 square feet of storage space and completed in 1941, was soon taxed to capacity by the wartime output.

The executive team left behind under the leadership of John J. Quinn, to shoulder the burden of running the plant during the grueling years of war, suffered another casualty at this time in the death of W. A. Comer, superintendent of the bindery. Mr. Comer's passing occurred only a few months after he had assumed the duties of the late John Buckley. This development brought J. Herbert Bryan to the post of bindery superintendent.

News from overseas became more encouraging. In 1944, Rome fell to the Allies; D-Day saw American and British forces landing in Normandy, and in a matter of weeks,

Paris was liberated. But the final year of war was to call for unrelenting pressure on the part of the Allies on all fronts, including the one at home. War-born shortages and restrictions became, if anything, more severe as the nation became fully converted to an emergency footing.

In common with other business firms, Quinn & Boden carried on despite these handicaps, and its officials were encouraged to find that even in wartime, business could show a steady growth. The figures from 1934 through 1946 evidenced a progressive increase each year, with sales registering 160 per cent higher than in 1927, when the company celebrated its twenty-first anniversary.

The heart-lifting news of Germany's unconditional surrender came on May 7, 1945, and three months later Japan capitulated under the none-too-gentle persuasion of the A-bomb blasts on Hiroshima and Nagasaki. The war was over, but many of Quinn & Boden's employees were scattered throughout the world in the various theaters of war. It was well into 1946 before the last of the men and women who had joined the armed forces returned to their jobs in the Rahway plant. Those who did not return are remembered and honored in the hearts of their colleagues.

It was early in the postwar period that another major change took place in the firm's executive echelons. Having brought the business safely through the heavy weather of a world war, John J. Quinn announced his retirement as president in October, 1946, and became chairman of the board. His successor was his younger brother James T. Quinn, who is president of the company today. Young

Quinn doffed his naval uniform for civilian attire as speedily as possible to return to the pressing duties that awaited him in the head office.

With the lifting of the wartime building ban, the company began construction of another warehouse. This one was completed in 1949, but it had scarcely been put to its intended use when the steady increase in business demanded more space for production, and the new warehouse was diverted to that purpose in the early 1950's.

Tragedy again befell the Quinn & Boden executive staff in 1951 with the passing of John J. Quinn at the age of sixty-nine. He left as his legacy a tradition of wise, farseeing business acumen, as his father had done. And his younger brother was well grounded in the know-how of directing the rapidly growing business.

A new executive staff was appointed in the same year: Malcolm S. Kerr, a certified public accountant formerly with W. C. Heaton & Co., joined Quinn & Boden as comptroller.

Albert F. Goetz was made assistant secretary. A graduate of the Wharton School of the University of Pennsylvania in 1934, Mr. Goetz came to Rahway in 1947 after twelve years with the Haddon Craftsmen, of Camden, New Jersey, where he had been assistant comptroller before joining the U.S. Army for a three-and-one-half-year stint during World War II.

Otto H. Muller, who joined the company in 1935 as a printing and binding estimator in charge of all estimating and billing, was elected to the Board of Directors in 1951. He continued to serve also as secretary of the firm, a post he assumed in 1943. Previous to joining Quinn & Boden, he had spent thirteen years with J. J. Little & Ives, book manufacturers in New York City.

The 1951 changes saw J. Herbert Bryan elevated to the vice presidency in charge of overall production. He joined the firm in 1942 as assistant bindery superintendent. Subsequently he was made manager. Mr. Bryan had a varied career after graduation from the high school at Hempstead, Long Island, in 1925. To prepare for a banking career, he entered the employ of the Second National Bank of Hempstead in 1925, but later obtained a position with a construction firm, where he remained four years. In 1930, he became associated with the Country Life Press in Garden City, and had reached the post of assistant to the bindery superintendent when he resigned in 1942 to take a similar position with Quinn & Boden.

In recent years, one of the most important additions to the staff has been that of Leonard Blizard, a veteran designer well known in book-making circles for his superior skill. He formerly was connected with Henry Holt and with Whittlesey House, a subsidiary of McGraw-Hill, publishers, as production manager. Since 1952, Mr. Blizard has been associated with the company's New York City office, now located at 381 Fourth Avenue. His highly specialized art is devoted to the typographical and pictorial aspects of the many books offered to the firm for manufacture. He is responsible for type design and for the layout decision which can lift the printer's craft into the realm of art.

The New York office, an important liaison post between the Rahway plant and the publishers, today is under the direction of Russell McDonnell, sales manager. On his staff are John Sweeney, Michael Quinn II, a grandson of the founder, and Roy Hollingshead, Jr., a son of the bindery foreman at the Rahway plant.

Turning again to the physical aspects of the business, the story of Quinn & Boden in the closing years of its first half-century has been one of continuous growth. The need for more storage space again was in evidence in 1953, and before the close of 1954 another warehouse was completed. This was the fourteenth addition made within the past fifty years to the two original buildings in which Quinn & Boden started business.

The sixteen structures that comprise the plant today cover a frontage equivalent to three city blocks. More important, the possibilities for further expansion on the present site are not yet exhausted.

Production demands have taken over one storage house after another, crowding out the packaged books awaiting shipment or being held for safekeeping. The question as to where the process will end is dealt with in a later chapter.

To a significant degree, the half-century of development at the Rahway plant has followed the larger pattern of national growth, as the miracle of industrial America created wealth and quickened human enterprise.

The founder of the plant in 1906 could estimate his working floor space at 40,000 square feet. As the firm reaches its fiftieth anniversary, the domain of Quinn & Boden covers a territory more than six times as large, with buildings and a recreation club occupying some 248,000 square feet, and with an additional 30,000 square feet allotted to parking space.

Business-wise, the firm also can underline the past ten years as marking the greatest increase in sales in the history of the business. Were the founder to look in on the progress of his handiwork today, he should be well pleased with what "his boys" have accomplished. Certainly his spirit remains as an almost visible force in the plant's administration.

STARS AND ASTERISKS

• • • • • • • •

Of the many rewards offered by the business of printing books, say members of the Quinn & Boden team, one of the most enjoyable is that of meeting an author now and then. Although the publisher is the one who ordinarily maintains direct, day-to-day contact with the writers in his "stable," the exigencies of the publishing industry bring authors, with surprising frequency, in person to the plant where their books are being manufactured. As a result, over the years, the Rahway plant has played host to many of the shining lights in the literary firmament.

While the visits of these distinguished people were aimed principally at checking certain details with the proofroom, Quinn & Boden veterans recall more than a few authors who came on business and remained to watch, with keen fascination, the process of turning their own words into book form.

Al Hoehle, assistant foreman of the composing room, remembers the day in 1929 when Commander Edward

Ellsberg of submarine fame visited Rahway while the firm was printing his first volume, "On the Bottom." This was Ellsberg's own graphic account of the raising of the *S-51*, a submarine which sank in one hundred thirty-five feet of water, carrying its crew to slow death, after being rammed by a steamship off Block Island. He wanted to check first-hand with the proofroom on the technical terms he had used to describe the tools he invented for the purpose of raising the sub.

Commander Ellsberg was a remarkable person, quite aside from the immediate recognition his book won for him as a master of vivid narrative. By special Act of Congress, he had been awarded the Distinguished Service Medal, the first time such an honor was accorded for peacetime service.

When word got around that the Commander was in the building, those who could leave their jobs for a moment scrambled to get a glimpse of him—and a few of the fortunate obtained autographs with which to impress the folks at home.

Alexander Woollcott, of the rapier wit and cleverly turned phrase, was another author who infused an otherwise routine Quinn & Boden working day with glamor, when he made his appearance at the plant during the manufacture of a second edition of "The Woollcott Reader" in 1935. The firm already had printed some 67,500 copies of the first edition, and now had 15,000 more on the presses.

Before driving back to New York that afternoon, the

pudgy author climbed the Pennsylvania Railroad's steep embankment near by to read the company's list of current books and authors emblazoned in a huge electric sign on top of the plant. A broad smile creased Woollcott's plump, round face as his own name met his gaze alongside the title of his latest book in the process of manufacture.

But most important of all, and best remembered by Quinn & Boden employees, was the evening author Carl Sandburg came from New York to entertain the plant personnel at the Cue-Bee Club. He brought along his guitar and they say he was in good voice as he sang many of his ballads and told some of his experiences, his research problems, and how he came to write the story of Abraham Lincoln.

It was called Carl Sandburg Night, and an estimated four hundred people turned out to meet the famous author. Ralph Kocher, superintendent of the Rahway High School, Arthur Perry, superintendent of the grade schools, and Mayor John Barger were on the welcoming committee.

The makers of books learned that evening that the writers of books also have their problems. Mr. Sandburg, ever at home with the workers, directed his talk to them. He told how it took him over a quarter of a century to compile the data on Lincoln and an additional four years to write the volumes it required the Rahway plant such a short time to print.

With his characteristic simplicity of speech he told them how he fitted an attic room in his Harbert, Michigan, farmhouse with a stove, a cot, a few chairs, a lot of book shelves and a typewriter perched on a low table. He said in the first two years he went through more than a thousand books looking up material.

From April to October each year, day in and day out, he pounded out his thoughts on the typewriter. During the winter months he took his guitar from its peg on the wall and toured the country, partly for a change of scene, but principally to look in on libraries and private Lincoln collections throughout the United States.

To illustrate his talk he reached across the table at the Cue-Bee Club that night, picked up his guitar, glanced out over his audience as if to check on their wishes, then began one of a dozen or more of his versions of "Frankie and Johnnie." He selected the one best suited to his mixed group, gracing the more earthy passages with a kind of dignity.

Margaret McCarthy, secretary to the late Michael F. Quinn, remembered how he walked through the crowd in the assembly room, shaking hands with everyone and autographing books and papers. She recalled the easy swing of the troubadour and even more vividly, his courtly manner.

When Pearl Weller was asked if lengthy biographies such as Sandburg's portrait of Lincoln and similar tomes on the life of George Washington posed a problem in her proofreading department, she shook her head in disagreement. She said that while they require great concentration, she and her co-workers considered this routine. "Foreign-language books and medical and mathematical textbooks are much more of a challenge than trade volumes because of their technical phrasing," commented Miss Weller.

Since the Second World War, the Rahway plant has welcomed a steadily increasing volume of business in the textbook field, until today this type of work constitutes eighty per cent of the firm's output. The balance is in trade books.

Although textbooks seldom achieve large circulation at a single printing, their reprint orders mean steady business. At the same time such work demands accuracy of a high order from the personnel through whose hands these manuscripts must pass.

Something that is not generally realized about textbooks is that their production must meet certain deadlines. A newly issued text must reach the market not only in time to be recommended by professors for their students in the fall, and to be purchased by the latter for use in classes; it must be in the hands of the professors for summer reading. Therefore tight scheduling is demanded of Quinn & Boden in this type of production.

An example of the moderately technical, highly accurate work the firm is required to do is the three-volume Martindale-Hubbell Law Directory, which must be brought up to date each fall. This huge compendium is considered something of a bible in legal circles, since it lists the new laws enacted by the various states and carries the biographies and addresses of lawyers throughout the country and other data essential to the legal profession.

Requiring even greater technical skill in their preparation are such surgical and medical tomes as Sterling Bunnell's "Surgery of the Hand," with its color plates and complex annotations, published by J. B. Lippincott & Co., or the "Merck Index," with its tabulation of all the known drugs.

The contents of such books must be checked and rechecked many times, and those responsible for their accuracy must have a working knowledge of each subject dealt with, which can only be acquired by years of application to this type of work.

A glance through the company's voluminous file of letters of appreciation, from both authors and publishers, bears out this contention. Horatio C. Wood, Jr., an editor of the "U.S. Dispensatory," expressed his gratitude "for careful and intelligent proofreading of highly technical material." And Arthur W. Ham congratulated a number of departments when he wrote:

"I think you have done an absolutely wonderful job on my volume on 'Histology.' The illustrations are beautifully reproduced. You could not have possibly made the book more attractive." And Kenneth Maxcy, one of the contributing authors to Dubos' "Bacterial and Mycotic Infections of Man," had this to say:

"Please accept my congratulations on the splendid job of composition that you have done."

Dr. N. Chandler Foot, who wrote "Identification of

Tumors," sent along his congratulations to the compositor as well as to the proofreaders. Praising the latter, he said the errors he normally expected were so few that they were doubly hard to detect, and complimented the proofroom on its concentration and infinite patience.

Thomas V. Moore, of the Department of Psychology at the Catholic University of Washington, who authored "Principles of Ethics" was brief but cogent in his praise: "Excellent proofreading."

Miss Weller says that some of these thank-you notes are simply routine messages from appreciative authors and publishers, but others are "praise from Caesar," as in the case of Louis Untermeyer, who could not tolerate errors. His letter of thanks, for this reason, is a treasured Quinn & Boden memento. It reads in part:

"The front matter of my 'Modern American Poetry' is flawless. I found the composition and proofreading extremely good, the best of any of my books."

Poet e. e. cummings was another in somewhat the same category, in that he preferred to use no capital letters and had other little peculiarities of style. On receiving the galleys of his "Fifty Poems," he wrote the Rahway plant:

"Congratulations—you've done a superb piece of work. Most of the mistakes are my own."

Says Miss Weller, "There are times, after particularly trying days, when a glance through the files of thank-you notes makes you feel that all the effort expended is very much worth while."

The reputation the Rahway plant has gained for its highly professional and accurate work in this department was earned through a well-thought-out plan of training prospective proofreaders after they finish high school. It requires anywhere from six to eight years to perfect a reader.

To hear these boys and girls reading copy to the proofreaders is not unlike listening to a couple of Egyptologists deciphering hieroglyphics chiseled on the walls of the Pyramids thousands of years ago. Especially is this true when they are reading such manuscripts as Addison's "X-Ray Diffraction for Metallurgists," which contains a maze of mathematical equations.

In the equally technical but wholly different field of writing, Alice Booth returned her galleys on "Music Index" with this note:

"I can't let this 'Index' go by without saying that never in my life have I seen a piece of narrow-measure copy set up with such perfect typography. In addition to being correct, it is beautifully spaced. This is most difficult work, being in what amounts to four languages, with varying styles of setting for different things. Inconsistencies were caught instantly. It was really wonderful work."

Howard Mumford Jones had this to say when his "Major American Writers" was completed:

"Congratulations to the printers on such a painstaking job on this volume. I have never in my experience had such painstaking care given any manuscript, or worked with such miraculously excellent proof."

Authors of trade books are equally appreciative of Quinn & Boden's careful handling of their product. James Joyce, who wrote "Finnegans Wake" in 1944, sent these words of praise to his publishers, Harcourt, Brace & Co.:

"My thanks for the valuable cooperation to those who have edited and set this recalcitrant piece." And Christopher Morley was another author who expressed his appreciation to the same publishers for the excellence of his "Thorofare," written in 1942.

Benjamin Brawley wrote, "Thanks to the printer for his fine handling of a difficult dialect." Robert Blake had words of praise, too, for the manufacture of "I'll Take the High Road."

The transition from trade to textbooks has been a gradual one at Quinn & Boden. For over fifteen years they have been cultivating the latter type of business, yet while scientific publications now far outbalance romance, biography, and mystery volumes, their current roster of fiction writers reads like "Who's Who."

That prolific British storyteller, Nevil Shute, whose output is published by William Morrow and Co., has been on the Quinn & Boden list for many years. In 1955, "The Breaking Wave" was printed in Rahway, and "Beyond the Black Stump" came off the presses early in 1956.

Erle Stanley Gardner was a boon to both publishers and printers back in the depression days. William Morrow and Co. tell of an incident in 1932 when they almost turned away the then unknown writer of whodunits, who in later years was to become the phenomenally prolific, supersuccessful creator of the Perry Mason series. The publisher's editorial staff reasoned that too many detective stories were flooding the American market at that time, and decided to hold off for six months.

It was Gardner's provocative title, "The Case of the Velvet Claws," later printed at the Rahway plant, that first attracted the staff's attention, and the reading matter completely changed their opinion. It has been said that his output could keep several printing houses busy at one time. It is claimed also that Gardner once produced 235,000 words in a single month. He has the kind of mind that can work simultaneously on two novels, an article and a short story. Many of his books have been printed in Rahway.

Rupert Hughes is another star-dusted name on the company's roster of authors. Much of his work was in research, and his biography of George Washington reveals his painstaking search for facts. His "F.B.I. Girl," published after the Second World War, was a novel based on his first-hand knowledge of how foreign agents infiltrated government departments.

One of Quinn & Boden's war problems was Marion Hargrove's "See Here, Private Hargrove," printed in 1942, when the staff was going off to battle. It sold well over 300,000 copies.

Pearl Buck's name is also on the company's "great author" list. Her first novel, "The Good Earth," was printed at Rahway. Others in the years that followed were James Hilton's "Lost Horizon"; Enid Bagnold's "National Velvet"; Wendell Willkie's "One World"; Robert Frost's "Complete Poems," and the steadily increasing output of Thomas Merton, which included "The Seven Storey Mountain," "No Man Is an Island," "Ascent to Truth," "The Last of the Fathers," and the "Sign of Jonas."

Thousands of trade and scientific volumes line ceiling-high bookshelves in the rooms of the Quinn & Boden executives, giving the front offices the appearance of a well-appointed library. Glancing over the titles, the eye catches such technical subjects as "Servomechanism and the Regulating System," by Chestnut and Mayer; Fruton's "General Biochemistry"; "The Human Body and Its Functions," by Best and Taylor; Battelle's "Steel and Its Heat Treatment," the American Geographical Society's "Geography of the Northlands"; "Short Wave Wireless Communications" by Ladner Stone, and many other volumes similarly abstruse and esoteric.

In a section set aside for college textbooks are volumes entitled "Engineering Drawing and Geometry," by Hoelscher; Strahler's "Physical Geography"; "Physical Geology" by Longwell, Knopf, and Fint; Daniels' "Physical Chemistry"; and two volumes of Gilman's "Organic Chemistry," to enumerate a few.

Do the typesetters and proofreaders enjoy the stories they print? Do they add to their education by assimilating the knowledge in these text and medical manuscripts? They say no. Their concern is entirely with reproducing in type what the author has written. To that extent the task is a mechanical one; its pleasure for Quinn & Boden employees springs from the satisfaction of knowing that complimentary notes from pleased authors and publishers are truly deserved.

THIS IS THE TEAM

• • • • • • • •

No man," to quote Donne, "is an iland intire of it selfe." The man who runs a machine at Quinn & Boden by day is the same man who goes home to a wife and children at night, and the dreams, ambitions, and worries of the one are those of the other.

In a broad sense, that thought is the rock on which the firm's labor policy is founded—if the term "labor policy" may be applied to an establishment where the relationship between employer and employee is pretty much a family affair. In the words of Frank A. Milbauer, the company's director of labor relations, "Quinn & Boden believes that the good relationships which have been maintained for the past fifty years may best be ascribed to a way of thinking rather than to any single policy or project."

Only a personal visit to the plant in Rahway can bring home to the outsider the remarkably informal atmosphere of the place in which every man and woman contributing to the finished product shares the sense of personal dignity and worth engendered by doing his or her job well—and by having his or her importance recognized.

Employees are complex, the firm believes. Their reactions stem from a dual role that is constantly being played. Each is an individual and must be treated as such. Yet each is a member of several groups, whose interests and actions interact with his own. These include the work unit or crew, the union, the family, the community, the church. A realization of the existence of these varied facets of the same problem goes a long way towards achieving a balanced orientation in the job environment.

Naturally, various policies are planned and put through in an effort to express this approach in practical terms. Quinn & Boden's program is conducted on three levels: employee relations, carried on through the company's contacts with the union; supervisory relations; and public relations. By dividing them into these categories, the firm points out, "we do not neglect any group in the plant, nor do we forget that our company is itself a member of the community.

"By treating the union representatives with the respect which we expect from them; by dealing honestly and fairly; by living up to the spirit as well as the letter of all agreements, and by viewing the union as an ally in the business rather than an enemy, we have reached a sound level of relations in this sphere."

At Rahway, supervisors are a part of management. Their authority and responsibilities are carefully outlined. They are informed of the latest developments in the company through regular meetings. Their education is supplemented through training programs. Working through them, the company maintains daily contact with its employees.

Apart from the union, the company works directly with its employees through a variety of social, sports, and community activities. It maintains a Twenty-five Year Club for veterans in the organization, a social center known as the Cue-Bee Club, and holds annual Christmas parties for children of the men and women in the organization.

Keeping in mind that the relationship is always a two-way street, the company seeks to make employees better acquainted with the problems of management also.

To this end, it issues to each employee a handbook of rules and regulations when he first joins the team, and from time to time distributes other informational literature.

Throughout the year, the Industrial Relations Department is ready to consider every phase of any problem that might be presented. If there is something on an employee's mind, it is not too small to warrant consideration. It is not uncommon for the employees to bring their financial, legal, marital, medical and other difficulties to the firm's attention.

The company understands that men do not live in compartments. What happens at home cannot be divorced from and stand apart from what goes on at the office or plant. Unity of treatment begets unity of purpose.

Close working relationship between management and the unions in the Rahway plant is a tradition that goes back to the days when Michael F. Quinn and Benjamin Boden, before they became its founding partners, were among the organizers and first officers of the International Brotherhood of Bookbinders (A.F.L.).

Mr. Quinn, who then lived in Malden, Mass., was selected as the union's first vice president and national organizer when it was established in 1892. He traveled widely throughout the United States and Canada, with authority to organize and charter local unions in the cities he visited.

His efforts proved most successful, as he was instrumental in placing the international union at its outset on a firm foundation. His services, rendered to the union without personal remuneration, continued through 1900, six years before he entered business and himself became an employer.

Mr. Boden, who came from Brooklyn, New York, was selected by the union upon its organization as a member of the International Executive Council. In May, 1894, he assumed the office of International Vice President and served one term before his elevation to the office of International President. He was re-elected in 1896 and 1897, serving three full terms as head of the International Brotherhood of Bookbinders.

In fact, it may be said that the association of these two men as officers of a fledgling union was the principal factor in bringing them together as business associates a few years later, and thus in the founding of the Quinn & Boden firm.

Management and the unions, co-operating as a team, have done much in the half century of the company's existence to improve working conditions, particularly concerning wages and hours. It is difficult to believe, and for veterans of the industry to remember, that in 1907, the year after Quinn & Boden established their partnership, the average working week was approximately sixty hours long. This was considered general for the industry and, of course, applied to Quinn & Boden as well.

Working hours had been reduced to fifty-four a week by 1920, and to forty-eight in 1929. Thereafter, the decrease has been dramatically swift. Quinn & Boden pioneered in instituting the forty-hour week in 1939, and as have other leading industrial plants, it has been cutting the average employee's work-time gradually below that level since then, until at present the working week consists of 36¼ hours. In addition to this, its employees now receive eight paid holidays a year and three weeks' vacation.

The change in rates of pay since Michael F. Quinn and Benjamin Boden began operations also has been startling. Between 1907 and 1929, wages in the industry tripled, and advanced another twelve per cent from 1929 to 1940, when the average pay in the Quinn & Boden shop was $1.23¾ cents an hour.

Realizing that the future of the firm lay in and with the city of Rahway, Michael F. Quinn long ago took steps to make sure that Rahway's people would have the first opportunity at steady, well-paying jobs with his organization—and that the company in turn could count on a steady supply of trained labor.

To that end, while president of the Rahway Board of Education in 1924, he instituted a program under which high-school students in the city, as part of their vocational training, were permitted to do part-time work in the plant. The program, still in effect, has been so successful that many of the firm's younger employees, and some of its department heads, are men and women who began there as high-school trainees.

Once it obtains the kind of employees it wants, the company does its best to keep them, not only by making compensation and hours of work as attractive as possible, but by providing for leisure-time pursuits. One of its ventures in this direction has been the Cue-Bee Club, maintained as a center of social and community activity for the workers.

A large frame structure located handily to the main plant, the clubhouse was dedicated in 1935 to the memory of Michael F. Quinn. Employees' dances and dinners are held here, while the comfortably furnished clubrooms have radio and television, pool tables, shuffleboards, bowling alleys, a small library, and other facilities for after-hours relaxation.

Bowling is one of the favorite sports now. The company has two teams of championship caliber comprising both men and women. They bowl on alternate nights during the week and play together in competition on Saturday night.

An integral part of the company's labor philosophy is the belief that incentive, the hunger for recognition, the sense of well-being that comes from doing a satisfying as well as a satisfactory job, the feeling of belonging to the team, are as important to the worker as his pay.

In the Rahway plant these needs are met through a variety of means. Wherever possible, promotions are made from the ranks, by way of recognizing merit and promise among the work crews. Almost every foreman at Quinn & Boden's is a former shop hand.

Security being a further factor for making workers happy, the company provides for both life insurance and temporary disability benefits, based on each person's straight-time wages. Life insurance policies range from $2,000 to $5,000, and disability payments run up to $46 a week for 26 weeks, also depending on basic pay.

For example, an employee earning $55 to $64 weekly receives a $3,500 life insurance policy, plus a maximum of $245 insurance for surgical operations and up to $175 for surgical operations for dependents. All policies are provided by the company.

The prospective employee applying for a job, unless he or she has previous experience, is assigned to the department where he or she is most needed, depending on ability and aptitude. The number of openings for apprentices in any given department is governed by the contracts in which management has entered with the various plant unions.

To become a journeyman compositor, for instance, one is required to serve an apprenticeship of six years. This length of time is also required for electrotypers, while four years is the minimum for pressmen and bookbinders.

Each craft in the plant is represented by its separate union. Those at Quinn & Boden are the International Typographical Union, the Electrotypers and Stereotypers Union, the International Printing Pressmen and Assistants Union, and the International Brotherhood of Bookbinders.

The apprenticeship in these crafts, designed to turn out workmen who are not merely competent but highly skilled, is short compared to that of Quinn & Boden's proofreaders. The shortest period in which one of these extremely specialized workers has been fully trained is eight years.

Of the nearly 600 employees at the Rahway plant, 232 work in the bindery, 105 are in the composing room, 84 in the pressroom, 53 in the shipping department, and 53 in maintenance. The balance are executives and clerical help.

Loyalty to the company is a notable trait among Quinn & Boden employees, of whom a gratifyingly large number have made their work with the company a lifetime career. No less than 100 of them are veterans of twenty-five years of service or more. Forty-four have spent thirty years with the organization, seven of them over forty years, and five of them have checked off fifty years or more.

William Swearer holds the top service record of sixty-three years in the bindery department. He worked thirteen years in the Mershon plant and stayed on the job when Quinn & Boden took over. Lloyd C. Madden comes next, rounding out fifty-eight years with the Rahway plant. Another oldster in point of service is Henry Hulsman, of the pressroom, who celebrated his golden jubilee with the firm a year ahead of Quinn & Boden.

Another veteran, Jim Lints, of the composing room, has been with the organization since 1911, and is the son of Frank Lints, who was employed there as a bookbinder under the Mershon Co.

Lints is also topped in seniority of service by Frank Witheridge, now superintendent of the upper bindery, who has been a Quinn & Boden employee for forty-seven years.

A third veteran, although a youngster compared to Lints and Witheridge, deserves mention as an example of the length to which the company's practice of advancement from the ranks can carry promising employees. He is Richard Wade, who joined the firm in 1930 as a proof boy. Richard received $11 a week to start for carrying proofs and sorting slugs, when the working week was forty-four hours long.

Wade soon advanced to become an apprentice in the composing room, and upon completing his preliminary service, served as a journeyman both on the make-up bank and as a linotype operator. Returning from military service in 1946, he was sent for a time to the company's New York office, and came back to Rahway in May, 1953. Since then he has become general superintendent of the composing room and foundry.

Behind these stalwarts in the front ranks stand the younger men and women who eventually will take their places. When that time comes, they will be equipped to assume the responsibility without faltering, while those who step aside will be able to do so in the full assurance that one good man is handing the baton to another.

A TITLE GOES TO PRESS

• • • • • • • •

The process of producing a book is a fusion of widely assorted graphic arts and crafts. No one of them can bring about the end result without the help of all the others—from writing to typesetting to the proper mixing of inks, and without any one of them, the rest are set at naught.

Yet to the printer more than to any other artisan involved—with the possible exception of the publisher, whose path runs parallel in the adjoining field of policy—falls the lot of bringing these diverse skills to practical application, of making a visual harmony of the whole.

Creating a book, regardless of its nature, imposes a severe demand upon the artistic as well as the professional capacities of the man (or more frequently, as in this case, the firm) who produces it. The author's and publisher's names adorn the title page; that of the printer, appearing on the copyright page in the instances where it is used, will tell the world as long as the book endures, who gave it form, appearance, and character.

For Quinn & Boden, any one such project may take several months, once the author's copy, or typewritten text, has been submitted to them along with the publisher's specifications as to the book's format and the size and face of type to be used. The time consumed by the job is determined both by the length of the text and by the publisher's promptness in returning corrected proofs to the printer.

By way of example, the galley proofs of one title set by Quinn & Boden went out to the publisher for corrections on November 15, and it was the following April 19 when the book finally went to press. Yet the completed book was ready for distribution by the publisher on May 5. At the other extreme was a 256-page book for which the galley proofs were sent out for correction February 20, the final forms went to press March 19, and the whole job, for which the press run was 3,000 copies, went in book form to the publisher on March 27.

Some idea of what one such operation entails in the way of materials was evolved back in the twenties when Quinn & Boden printed the entire first edition of Sinclair Lewis's "Dodsworth," numbering 100,000 copies. The job required three carloads of paper, in sheets measuring 41 by 61 inches, 960,000 yards of thread, 50 pounds of glue, eight tons of binder's board, 10,000 yards of blue cloth, 500 pounds of black ink, and 50 pounds of orange ink.

In turning this book out, two of the Rahway plant's largest presses, printing 128 pages at a time, were kept busy night and day for fifteen days, along with two of its largest folding machines. The book, in its various stages, passed through about 120 different hands. If the copies were placed end to end, they would form a line 67,000 feet long. It would require four freight cars to ship the bound books, and if they were stacked one on top of the other, the pile would be 12,500 feet high, ten times the height of the Empire State Building.

From the very first step in the manufacturing process, when the number of pages a book will make is estimated, until the final one, when the bound copies are packed in cartons and shipped, the same fastidious standard of perfection which once prompted Michael F. Quinn to destroy the entire edition of a slightly imperfect book in the early days of the firm, prevails today at the Rahway plant.

Before the book is set up in type, it must be planned. This is primarily the publisher's function, but in carrying it out, the publisher leans heavily on what is often the longer and more varied practical experience of the printer. Thus it is that some of the outstanding book publishers frequently turn to the manufacturer for consultation before deciding on the format, selection of type best suited for the job, the grade and finish of paper, style of binding, and similar matters.

There are many functional considerations that go into producing a book. The extras which a printing house like Quinn & Boden seeks to add by way of making its books more interesting and attractive are often intangible; the free play of a craftsman's imagination, his love of a perfectly turned product, may contribute the sparkle, the winning touch of beauty, that might otherwise not have been there.

Once the size of the page and the style of type face have been decided upon, the author's typescript can be handed to the compositor to be set into type. This is done on an ingeniously designed machine, called a linotype, with a keyboard somewhat resembling a typewriter, which collates the matrices, or indented dies, of each letter in rapid succession until a whole line of the required length has been assembled and spaced, and then casts this line in a single piece, or "slug," of type metal to the page width.

When these lines of type have been set, all corresponding exactly to the lines of print which will appear on the page of the book, they are arranged together in order, face upward, within a metal tray known as a galley. Ink is rolled over their surfaces and a proof run off on proving paper so that the proofreaders, by comparing the proof with the author's copy, can catch and have the errors corrected.

After the galley proofs have been read and approved by the publisher and author, the type is made up into pages, proofs pulled, which are revised by the proofreaders, and then sent to the publisher for a final reading.

At this point the book's embellishments are designed and set into type: the half-title, title page, copyright page, dedication, foreword, and table of contents, if any. These, too, go in proof form to the publisher for verification.

All this shipping back and forth of proofs may seem to the layman like a great deal of lost motion, but it is part of the exactitude through which errors are kept to a minimum. It is next to impossible to produce a book that has not a single typographical error.

The next process is to "lock up" the type, either for printing from slugs or for plate-making. If the job is to print from type, it is locked firmly in a large steel frame, called a chase, which holds from 16 to 64 type pages, according to the size of the page, and then transferred to the pressroom. This is usually the procedure whenever the quantity to print is small.

When the amount is large enough, electrotypes or plastic plates are used. Electrotypes are made by using a vinylite mold of the original type and submerging it in a tank containing a copper sulphate solution, which then, by the process of electrolysis, deposits a thin copper shell on the surface of the mold. This shell is carefully removed from the mold and backed up with a molten lead alloy to reinforce it. The plate is then trimmed of surplus metal, the edges are beveled, and the lead backing shaved to its proper thickness.

Plastic plates are molded in much the same manner as the electrotypes, except that the printing surface is formed by a thick layer of vinyl-resin powder, which is forced into the mold under heat and pressure, the molds are removed, and the plate then trimmed, beveled, and shaved.

With the plate-making completed, the job is ready to "go to press." The plates are imposed in correct position on the platen, or bed, of the press, and then begins a long, laborious hand operation known as make-ready. This consists of leveling the plates by means of small pieces of paper placed between the platen and the plate, to compensate for any inequalities in the plate's surface. From two to eight hours are necessary for this, and the end result depends on how well this is done.

Once the make-ready is completed, actual printing begins. A series of distributing rollers spread ink across the surface of the plates as they move back and forth under them. After moving in one direction to pick up the film of ink, the bed carrying the plates moves back again beneath a large cylinder which revolves on its axle.

A single sheet of paper is carried by a set of grippers on the outer surface of the cylinder, and as the leading edge of the paper comes down into position against the leading edge of the printing plate, the cylinder drops slightly on its axle to press the paper against the inked surfaces of the type. The paper is released from the surface of the cylinder after being printed and is dropped on a delivery board, where the freshly printed sheets are piled. Meanwhile the cylinder has been raised again on its axle to permit the printing plate to travel back for another load of ink, and another sheet of paper is fed into the grippers on the cylinder's surface in order to repeat the process.

Different size presses are used, depending on the number of copies to be printed and the size of paper to be used. Quinn & Boden's pressroom is equipped with presses that will accommodate almost all sizes of paper standard with publishers.

Once the printed sheets are dry enough to be handled, they are taken to the bindery, where machines fold them into signatures of 16 or 32 pages each, this being governed by the weight of the paper.

The folding machine carries the flat sheet on tapes across a long, blunt-edged blade, which strikes the paper at the point at which a fold is desired, and thrusts the edge of the fold thus started in between two rollers with roughened surfaces. These press the paper between them so as to complete the fold and crease it. Another set of tapes then carries the paper across another blade and through another set of rollers to repeat the process. In a job calling for more than four folds, the paper is slit in two before the additional folds are made.

The bindery also sees to it that the end leaves, which later are to be attached by paste to the inside covers, are fastened to the first and last signatures of the book before it is sewn together. The sewn volumes, after being smashed, glued, and then trimmed to the desired size, are next rounded and backed, so as to give the familiar concave effect to the fore edge and the convexity to the back which makes the book fit better in its case. After the book has been rounded, a final reinforcement is given it in the form of strips of paper and crash, a type of wide-meshed muslin, which run vertically along the spine and extend outward on either side. These are now pasted into place.

Cases, or covers, for the books are made separately as a unit. The first step is to cut sheets of binder's board, a composition material, to the proper size for the front and back covers. Either cloth or paper, depending on the quality and price of the book, is used to cover these boards, again being pasted in place so as to lap over on the inner edges.

In the stamping department, the title, name of the author, and that of the publisher are stamped on the cloth surface of the case, across the spine, and either the title or a decorative device is also stamped across the front before the cases are sent to an assembling point to meet the forwarded books.

This point is known as the casing-in department. The books get a last coat of paste on the end papers before they are inserted in the cases by machine. They then are held tightly in clamps overnight for the paste to set and dry.

Every one of the processes described thus far is subject to careful inspection as the stage is completed, so that if the first specimens coming through reveal flaws, the trouble can be corrected without serious loss of time and material.

The paper book-jacket, or wrapper, as it is sometimes called, provides the finishing touch for the book. To catch the eye of the reading public and make a favorable first impression in competition with other books on the retailer's shelves, the jacket is designed as strikingly as possible. Often it is printed in a variety of colors and the most emphatic of display type to achieve something of the effect of a poster, care being taken at the same time to avoid the garish.

Printing books, in the half century which has elapsed since the company's founding, has become largely a mechanical process. But care and attention to detail in the control of those processes is required to maintain a high standard of production in which workmen as well as executives can afford to take pride.

NEW DEVICES AND TECHNIQUES

Despite television, radio, and the many other distractions which now compete for the attention of the American reader, there is a continuing demand for specialized books. The result has been to strain to the limit the capacity of book manufacturing concerns, and to keep them constantly alert for methods of speeding production as well as improving quality.

In the race to maintain top efficiency of operation, it is imperative to weigh the possibilities of new devices and techniques with relation to the individual bookmaker's needs. Only when one compares the relatively enormous output of modern manufacturing methods with that of the ones in use in 1906, and considers the many improvements in the quality of that output, does the spectacular extent of the change wrought by fifty years become apparent.

That first small press used by the Mershon brothers does more than symbolize the firm's reverence for a great tradition. It demonstrates, in a way that words cannot, the vast span of progress between the company of today and its beginnings.

The degree of change which has come about in each of the many operations involved in bookmaking varies with its adaptability to machine work and with the effectiveness of the devices already being used in it. The highest tribute, for example, which can be paid to the ingenuity and foresight of Ottmar Mergenthaler, inventor of the Linotype, is that the machines of that name still being used by the firm today, modern though they are, differ surprisingly little in basic operation from those used in 1906.

Linotype metal nowadays is melted in electrically heated pots, but except for this change and an assortment of new type-faces, an old-time compositor might wander into the composing room tomorrow and find himself quite at home.

Hand setting of type, except for specialized work involving a great number of technical symbols or foreign-language copy, gave way to machine setting considerably before Quinn & Boden went into business.

During the past fifteen years due to the transition from trade books to textbooks, the Monotype Department, so essential in the manufacture of the complicated and highly technical engineering, medical, and foreign language books, has been greatly expanded. This method approaches hand type in that the characters are cast individually instead of a line at a time. This allows for the insertion of diversified characters, symbols, and accents.

New Devices and Techniques

Perhaps the greatest change in production methods and equipment has come about in the company's foundry since the Second World War. While the firm still uses electrotypes for certain purposes, it is estimated that ninety per cent of its plate-making now is done in plastics. A great deal of this change-over has occurred in the last five years.

For nearly two decades beginning in 1923, the firm imported from Poland a material known as ozocerite for use in the molding of electrotype plates. The war cut off this source of supply, and the foundry turned to American-made synthetics. These proved unsatisfactory, since they developed honeycombs in the face of the plate.

The firm next turned to a form of vinylite, which has been used successfully in electrotyping here for more than a decade. Although its initial cost is high, it has proved satisfactory.

Vinylite is distinguished by one of the peculiar characteristics of plastics, in that it has a "memory." An impression taken in it changes the molecular structure of the material itself, so that even after it has been pressed out smooth again, the type shadows may still be seen in it.

The plastic plates now used by the foundry in place of electrotypes display the same peculiarity. If they become battered, the application of a little heat (merely running a lighted match across the surface will do it) causes the flattened type to leap out on the surface just as it was before.

New Devices and Techniques

Use of plastics in plate-making is one of the ways in which efficiency of production has been increased to combat the rising costs of labor and materials. In the latter part of 1953, the foundry introduced another major innovation. Until then it had employed electric generators to provide current for the electrolytic process by which a copper shell is deposited on the mold to form the face of the electrotype. At that time the generators were replaced by rectifiers, which do exactly the same job, but take up about one-tenth the space. In addition to being space-savers, rectifiers require little upkeep, in that they have few movable parts to get out of order.

These and other transitions which have occurred in the foundry in the past thirty years have made for a cleaner and pleasanter place in which to work, besides contributing to a better product.

The pressroom, heart of the printing operation, also has seen numerous changes and improvements at Quinn & Boden during the half-century now ending. Fast-drying inks and speedier presses have done much to increase the rate of production, simplify the work involved, and reduce operational costs.

By far the most sensational change in this department has been the introduction of the offset process, a form of lithography, by which an inked impression is transferred to the paper from a rubber-covered blanket, thus eliminating many of the intermediate steps involved in letterpress printing.

"Offset," in another sense, used to be one of the banes

of a printer's existence, since it once meant only the smudge left when a freshly printed sheet of paper came in contact with another sheet. This has been a problem with which the industry, and Quinn & Boden, have sought to cope for many years. The answer has been found in inks which dry quickly through the introduction of compounds into the ink itself, rather than through the application of external drying agents such as heat, which have proved too slow.

Chemical compounds are used to produce flash-drying of ink in printing on heavily coated gloss paper, but for average work the Rahway plant now uses concentrated cobalt. This hastens drying by oxidation.

Years of laboratory work and experimentation have gone into the search for more efficient types of press rollers. So-called rubber rollers, made with the synthetic neoprene, have proved highly efficient in offset lithography. However, for letterpress work the company has found nothing so far to surpass the glue and glycerine rollers that have been in use for almost a century.

Quinn & Boden also has experimented with rubber printing plates, in the hope of cutting down on the time required for make-ready. It was found, however, that rubber as a substitute for metal or plastic has not yet reached the stage where it can be used for quality printing.

In fact, any method that eliminates make-ready by avoiding either interlay or overlay must be predicated on absolute perfection of type and plates before they are delivered to the pressroom.

Another department at Rahway which bears very little resemblance to its appearance fifty years ago is the bindery. The transition here has been a gradual one, as first one type of machine and then another was developed to do away with what originally was largely hand work. In the last thirty years particularly, great strides have been made in mechanization of this department, due to competition among machinery manufacturers for the bookbinders' business.

In the folding operation, for instance, the machines now in use can produce two to three times as many sheets as was possible during the early years of the company.

Several new high-speed "N-quad" folders have been installed in this department recently, and last year a large Bennett folding-machine was added to its equipment. There are only six or seven of the latter in this country. In addition to these, several high-speed job folders are employed.

Of course production depends to a great extent on the weight of the paper used. Certain lightweight papers slow down the folding operation to some degree, but without exception the process has been speeded substantially by the use of modern machinery.

In the next operation, that of pasting the end sheets to the first and last signatures of a book, a recent improvement has been made on the older type tipping machine. While fundamentally similar, it has greatly increased the productive capacity of this operation.

Transition in types of machinery in the gathering department has been very gradual. The greatest improvement here has been the introduction of new, strong, lightweight metals for the construction of the big, cumbersome machines required, with the result that they can operate at considerably greater speeds.

In the sewing department, the greatest change was the straight-needle machine, which was gradually installed by Quinn & Boden in the early 1930's.

For years the standard machine in the smashing department was a four-post press for compressing the books before trimming. This was superseded by a machine with a belt conveyor, which also increased production. Still more recently, a new machine has been developed which combines the nipping and gluing in one operation.

In this machine the books are piled on their spines into a hopper feed, and fed in one at a time. The books are first jogged on their backs to get the signatures even, then given a nip along the back, where they are sewed. Next they are given a much harder nip, after which they are jogged again before passing over a roller, where glue is applied to the backbone.

The task of rounding and backing has changed little in its essential features over the years, but it has progressed from a hand-powered machine to a high-speed semi-automatic operation.

Lining-up, not so long ago, was entirely manual. In recent years, machines have been developed to take over a large portion of this operation. There are many large volumes that still require the use of the old hand methods, however.

In cutting boards for the covers, or cases, as they are called, the full sheet of cardboard originally was cut into strips and then chopped separately into individual pieces of the size needed for the finished cover. The next advance was a machine to combine these operations, so as to strip and chop at the same time.

This device has been improved still further in recent years by the addition of an automatic feeder, which takes the boards directly from the skid-load just as they are received from the supplier and strips and chops in a continuous operation. The new automatic board cutter installed at Rahway in 1956 can cut considerably more than was possible on the old hand-fed machine.

There have been very few developments in case-making machinery until recent years. There are two types of equipment: one that feeds individual pieces of cloth for short-run work, and another which feeds the cloth from a roll in a continuous web for high-speed production on large editions.

New skills must constantly be developed in the handling of new machines as technological progress continues. The current demand for more and more pre-printed covers is creating an example of this at the present time in one of the final operations of bookmaking. Three machinery manufacturers are each developing machines they hope will produce covers from single pieces at about three times the speed now possible. These machines are expected to go into production shortly.

The addition of electric motors has been the only radical change in the company's stamping presses. Since then, certain refinements have been added, but the improvement in materials, notably ink, metallic foils and pigment leaf, has been chiefly responsible for speeding up production in this department.

While casing-in, the operation of placing covers on books, is now handled entirely by machinery, the job of building-in, which follows that of casing, has been done in much the same way ever since bookbinding began. It consists of placing the cased books between flat boards which have a beaded edge to form the hinge of the cover.

Still between boards, the book is clamped in place under heavy pressure to permit thorough drying of the paste which holds it within the covers. This process, until a few years ago, took from twelve to twenty-four hours, but now it can be done in a few seconds, with the aid of new devices called building-in and drying machines, which apply heat together with compression.

When they emerge from this machine, the books are ready for examination and jacketing, after which they are placed on skids or in cartons preparatory to shipment or storage.

Even this latter phase of the operation has been mechanized. A sealing machine closes and fastens the top and bottom of the shipping carton in one continuous operation. In some instances, a machine tight-wraps one or more books in packages up to five inches thick, doing automatically what once was performed manually.

The jackets which now go on books came into general use as a sales-promotion device prior to 1920. Their evolution provides an interesting demonstration of the limits set by practical considerations on technological advance.

The first jackets for trade books were plain printed wrappers, in two colors at the most, and a far cry from the showy creations which try to outdo each other now on the book-sellers' shelves. Mechanically, the first improvement in jacket manufacture was the application of a coat of varnish to impart a rich gloss to its surface and preserve it somewhat against the wear and tear of handling. This, however, also brought its drawbacks, since varnish dries slowly.

In keeping with the long-established American business tradition that each problem, by inspiring its own answer, creates a new advance, this final phase of the book-finishing process has been worked out successfully at Quinn & Boden through the use of compressed air.

There was a time when completed books were hauled from the jacketing department to the warehouse on hand trucks. Now pert-looking little electric dollies do the same job faster and easier. They typify the fast-moving world in which this fast-moving firm operates.

Handling, incidentally, is one of the non-productive cost items which has increased steadily in comparative importance on the firm's balance sheet, as mechanization has cut the unit cost of production operations. The extent to which full automation can benefit the book-manufacturing business is strictly limited, since this is essentially a craft process. For the high quality and the profitable volume of its product, the Rahway plant places ultimate dependence on skills which its employees have taken many years to acquire. They will always constitute its most valuable asset.

BLUEPRINT FOR THE FUTURE

• • • • • • • •

Conservative business practices, new production techniques, and a determination to keep a step or two ahead in the race to provide the latest and best in equipment has been Quinn & Boden's blueprint for expansion during the past fifty years.

The loyalty and morale of its over 600 people, from officers to proof boys, have never been higher as the firm reaches its golden anniversary. Now, as in the past, it recognizes this general enthusiasm as one of its prime assets. Every effort is made today to sustain this individual interest on the part of each person in the Rahway plant.

In recent years, conservatism and recognition of the need for progress have made a working team (not nearly as paradoxical as it may seem) in the Quinn & Boden front office. Their joint effort has resulted in the carefully-thought-out, long-range planning responsible for the most significant shift in production emphasis in the company's history. This is the complete about-face from a preponderance of trade-book printing to a preponderance of textbooks.

As mentioned earlier, during the twenties, and well into the depression era, the company had an output made up approximately of eighty per cent trade books and twenty per cent textbooks. As recently as 1950, the reverse percentages held good. Today, the ratio of trade books is down to ten per cent.

The Second World War "triggered" the last phase of this changeover. First, it opened the way to the tremendously rapid growth of the television industry, which more than any one factor has changed the entertainment habits of the American nation. Second, it set off the greatest building-and-baby boom this country has ever seen.

Motion pictures have not been alone in feeling the effects of television's inroads. Reading for pleasure, in the form of novels and allied trade books, has taken a distinct setback, so that while as many titles are being published as ever, the number of copies being printed per title is drastically reduced.

A parallel to this change, although not related directly to it, has been the postwar movement of literally millions of families into millions of new ranch-type and split-level homes, generally in hitherto undeveloped areas. And since these are usually young families with relatively large numbers of children, multitudes of new schools have had to be built, and are still being built, to accommodate them. New schools call for new equipment—notably textbooks.

The late John J. Quinn, whose foresight reached far beyond the margins of his account books, would have been too modest to claim that he saw these developments coming, but as a shrewd businessman, he could spot a trend as quickly as the next one. Prior to his retirement as president in 1946, and as board chairman from that time until his death in 1951, he was instrumental in helping to steer more and more of Quinn & Boden's production into the textbook field. His younger brother and successor, James T. Quinn, who joined in the decision to carry the shift to its logical conclusion, has had every reason to be satisfied with it, and to carry the policy forward.

While pushing deeper into its newly chosen area, the firm has been able to retain the advantages of diversification which it enjoyed when the positions of trade books and textbooks were reversed. The chronic ups and downs of business seldom are likely to affect both branches of the printing industry simultaneously, so that each branch can serve as a cushion for the other.

"In fact," comments the present head of the firm, "we look forward to enjoying a greater degree of stability in textbooks than trade books have ever given us.

"We look forward with a great deal of confidence to the future," he asserted. "Most of our good publishing friends seem to think that the next five to ten years will see the greatest increase in history in the textbook field. The increase in the number of elementary and high schools will account for only part of it. Remember, more and more people are feeling the need to broaden their education, through graduate work, adult schools, and other means. Textbooks will be in demand—big demand—as long as this country keeps on growing. We have faith that it will keep on."

As evidence of that faith, Quinn & Boden even now is planning a very considerable expansion of its production facilities, so that the first years of its second half-century will be marked by a building program dwarfing the original facilities of 1906.

Because the company has nearly exhausted the space available to it in the vicinity of the present manufacturing plant, the new storage units will have to be built in other parts of Rahway. This will be the first time the firm has found it necessary to divide its storage facilities geographically on any sort of permanent basis. So far it has been able to concentrate its manufacturing operations in the single complex of sixteen buildings that now comprise the Rahway plant.

To prophesy without knowledge, it has been pointed out, is dangerous as well as foolish, but on the basis of past experience and the safeguards the company has tried to maintain as a result of that experience, Quinn & Boden feels reasonably well prepared to cope with whatever situations the future may present.

In time of war, it helped meet the need for vast amounts of printed matter, for the information of both the armed forces and the home front. At the same time it contributed to the country's actual front-line defense its full quota of young men trained in the old-fashioned virtues of doing the job assigned to them—of doing the job willingly, thoughtfully, with care, and without undue complaint.

These are the bedrock principles laid down by the founder—the kind which make for long life in any business, and for the respect of a company's clients and competitors. The firm values them and insists on their observance principally because the company takes a craftsman's professional pride in a product that speaks well for his work.

The Quinn & Boden imprint, which used to stamp all the books printed at Rahway, can still be found on volumes in libraries and on the shelves of bookstores throughout the world. Many an American tourist has picked them up in London, Cairo, Buenos Aires, Melbourne. They are in schoolrooms and in laboratories where scientists toil to bring atomic equations into awesome reality, the texts and tables carrying out faithfully their heavy burden of dependability.

While these are reassuring evidences of sound business principles, the firm places high on its list of assets the friendly relationships it has maintained for so long with its clients—a distinguished cross-section of the publishing industry.

It is through the continuation of this service that the Rahway plant looks forward to its solid development in the future. For while publishing involves a greater than ordinary element of risk and has had more than its share of casualties during periods of economic stress, in the main it has proved a remarkably durable business.

A handful of America's publishing houses go back to the days when the business was in its infancy, and printer and publisher were virtually indistinguishable. Among these are two of the Rahway plant's old customers, the J. B. Lippincott Co., founded in 1792, and John Wiley and Sons, Inc., founded in 1807.

Many distinguished houses with which the Rahway organization has done mutually satisfactory business for long periods can also look back over a century or more of publishing history. These include Dodd, Mead and Co., founded in 1839, and the equally well-known publishing firm of Henry Holt and Co., which has only ten years to go before reaching its century mark. Oxford University Press, whose publishing history goes back four centuries, also has been a valued customer since Quinn & Boden's earliest days.

While standing in proper awe of such veterans, Quinn & Boden at this point can share a certain camaraderie with other publishing houses which are junior to it. The great book firm of McGraw-Hill, Inc., for instance, began business when the people in Rahway already had three years of hard going behind them. Toward other publishing clients such as Harcourt, Brace and Co., and William Morrow and Co., which came into the field when the present century was in its teens and even later, the firm can afford a feeling of almost fatherly interest as well as pride in their success.

For these are the people—these and many others now in the publishing business or yet to enter it—with whom Quinn & Boden look forward to sharing their second half-century in that close and truly unique partnership which always has marked the association between printer and publisher.

To each of its friends, the many suppliers, the citizens and officials of Rahway whose generous co-operation has contributed in great measure to its success, Quinn & Boden extend grateful recognition.

Now, as the firm starts rounding the turn toward the first century milestone, it is with a feeling of assurance that the journey ahead will prove as stimulating as the past fifty years have been mutually rewarding.

HONOR ROLL—1906–1956

• • • • • • • •

Contributing also to Quinn & Boden's growth during the years have been many other individuals in addition to those mentioned in this history. To list them all would require a volume much larger than the present book.

To the following, the firm remains forever grateful for their assistance, especially during the early years.

Administration and Sales

Harry E. Wade, sales and composing room
James B. Mershon, sales
Edgar L. Wagoner, sales and composing room
William Buckley, sales
Howard Wagoner, sales and estimating
Marcus Bradford, assistant treasurer
Melvin Bailey, sales and vice president
Arthur Braunworth, sales and vice president

Composing Room

William Brown, foreman
Charles Schweitzer, foreman
Charles Koops, foreman
George Irving, foreman
David MacIntosh, head reader
Harry Brown, estimator and foreman
John Moran, Sr., foreman
James Quinn, estimator

Foundry

William Hornby, foreman
John J. Halley, foreman
Robert Hornby, co-foreman
George Crowell, co-foreman
William Harding, foreman

Press Room

Henry Haefle, foreman
Richard Walsh, foreman
Michael Callahan, foreman
James Boice, foreman
William Bennett, stock man
William Somerindyke, plate vault

Bindery

John Duff, foreman
Harry Winchester, foreman
Edward Metz, foreman stamping department
William Ader, foreman stamping department
Peter Becker, head stamper
Roy Clark, sheet man

Shipping

Walter Moore, foreman
Joseph Cogan, foreman
Rudolph Buckman, foreman
Mark Connor, foreman

Maintenance

George Squier, supervisor
Charles Darling, supervisor
Michael Connors, supervisor
Isaac Williams, supervisor

TWENTY-FIVE YEAR CLUB

• • • • • • • •

The loyalty of the employees, as well as the satisfaction they realize from their respective occupations, is evidenced by the fact that over fifty per cent of the staff have been with the company more than ten years, and over twenty per cent have a record of twenty-five or more years.

NAME	YEARS OF SERVICE
WILLIAM SWEARER—*Bindery*	63
LLOYD C. MADDEN—*Bindery*	58
HENRY HULSMAN—*Pressroom*	51
ROY OSBORNE—*Bindery*	51
JACOB REPCKA—*Bindery*	51
JOHN GASSER—*Bindery*	48
FRANK WITHERIDGE—*Bindery*	48
MARGARET DANIELS—*Bindery*	46
FREDERIC H. MARTIN—*Pressroom*	46
CARRIE LARSON—*Bindery*	45
JAMES D. LINTS—*Composing Room*	45

Twenty-Five Year Club

NAME	YEARS OF SERVICE
Anna Brunt—*Bindery*	42
Alfred J. Hoehle—*Composing Room*	39
Clifford Moorehead—*Foundry*	39
Clifton Smith—*Pressroom*	39
Roy Hollingshead—*Bindery*	38
John V. Nourse—*Office*	38
Mazie Owens—*Bindery*	38
Peter Romeo—*Bindery*	38
Andrew Semple—*Composing Room*	38
Ethel Hoagland—*Bindery*	37
Margaret C. McCarthy—*Office*	37
Hilda Fischer—*Bindery*	36
Charles Serson—*Bindery*	36
Margaret Egan—*Proofroom*	35
Edna Hedeman—*Proofroom*	35
Edith Henrich—*Bindery*	35
Leland D. Martin—*Bindery*	35
Pearl M. Weller—*Proofroom*	35
John Cahill, Sr.—*Pressroom*	34
Lenwood Hughes—*Shipping Dept.*	34
Edith Kay—*Proofroom*	34
William B. McCaskill—*Foundry*	34
Amil Borden—*Foundry*	33
Walter R. Christopher—*Bindery*	33
Margaret Hedrick—*Bindery*	33
Mildred Hennessey—*Bindery*	33
Michael A. Link—*Composing Room*	33

NAME	YEARS OF SERVICE
Percy W. McAvoy—*Foundry*	33
Florence O'Donnell—*Bindery*	33
Frank Savacool—*Pressroom*	33
Joseph Yashinovich—*Bindery*	33
Charles L. Carroll—*Bindery*	32
Joseph Davis—*Bindery*	32
Mae Feuchter—*Bindery*	32
William Gubas—*Bindery*	32
John F. Mooney—*Pressroom*	32
Julius V. Petrisin—*Bindery*	32
Annise R. Regensburg—*Bindery*	32
Harry R. Smith—*Pressroom*	32
Ida Swearer—*Bindery*	32
William H. Walker—*Bindery*	32
Charles H. Wier—*Bindery*	32
Bessie Nelson—*Bindery*	31
Andrew Peterson—*Bindery*	31
Charles Stevens—*Bindery*	31
Edward De Carlo—*Bindery*	30
George D. Heath—*Composing Room*	30
Andrew Medvigy—*Bindery*	30
Freda Mintel—*Bindery*	30
James Simpson—*Composing Room*	30
Carl Winters—*Composing Room*	30
James J. Finer—*Bindery*	29
Joseph Gere—*Pressroom*	29
Georgia W. Haggerty—*Proofroom*	29

Twenty-Five Year Club

NAME	YEARS OF SERVICE
THEODORE C. LITTELL—*Pressroom*	29
WILLIAM S. MASON—*Bindery*	29
ELIZABETH A. MOHR—*Bindery*	29
CATHERINE L. POLIN—*Bindery*	29
JAMES T. QUINN—*Office*	29
FREDERICK R. M. SHEPPARD—*Bindery*	29
ERNEST F. VEECK—*Pressroom*	29
ANNA BECK—*Bindery*	28
ELVA BETTLE—*Bindery*	28
HOWARD BORST—*Composing Room*	28
LEROY DONNELLY—*Pressroom*	28
JOHN J. GOULD—*Composing Room*	28
HARRY GREENE—*Composing Room*	28
ALFRED HEIDERE—*Pressroom*	28
LESTER LUDLOW—*Bindery*	28
WILLIAM J. RIEFLER—*Bindery*	28
THOMAS THOMPSON—*Bindery*	28
GEORGE VACHE—*Bindery*	28
GLENN WORMUTH—*Composing Room*	28
STEPHEN CEDERLE—*Bindery*	27
HELEN MALCOLM—*Bindery*	27
MILTON CRANS—*Bindery*	27
NORA DORSETT—*Bindery*	27
OWEN DOYLE—*Maintenance*	27
CHRISTIAN HENRICH—*Pressroom*	27
SYLVIA HEWITT—*Office*	27
JOHN LANG—*Pressroom*	27

NAME	YEARS OF SERVICE
MARY STINEMIRE—*Bindery*	27
JOSEPH SZEFCZYK—*Bindery*	27
RICHARD WADE—*Office*	27
STEPHEN WERBECK—*Composing Room*	27
ERNEST EINHORN—*Pressroom*	26
HARRY KENT—*Composing Room*	26
HENRY MILLER—*Bindery*	26
ALPHONSE CASEY—*Office*	25
ROBERT CLARK—*Bindery*	25
IDA LEWIS—*Proofroom*	25
MYRON PERNEY—*Composing Room*	25

Main gate to the office and plant as it appears today.

The office as it appeared in 1915, with M. F. Quinn at his desk.

John J. Quinn takes his place across the desk from his father.

MANUFACTURERS OF BO

A view of the old Mershon Company in 1906, the year M. F. Quinn and Benjamin Boden purchased the plant.

QUINN & BODEN CO
BOOK
MANUFACTURERS
BODEN CO
INC

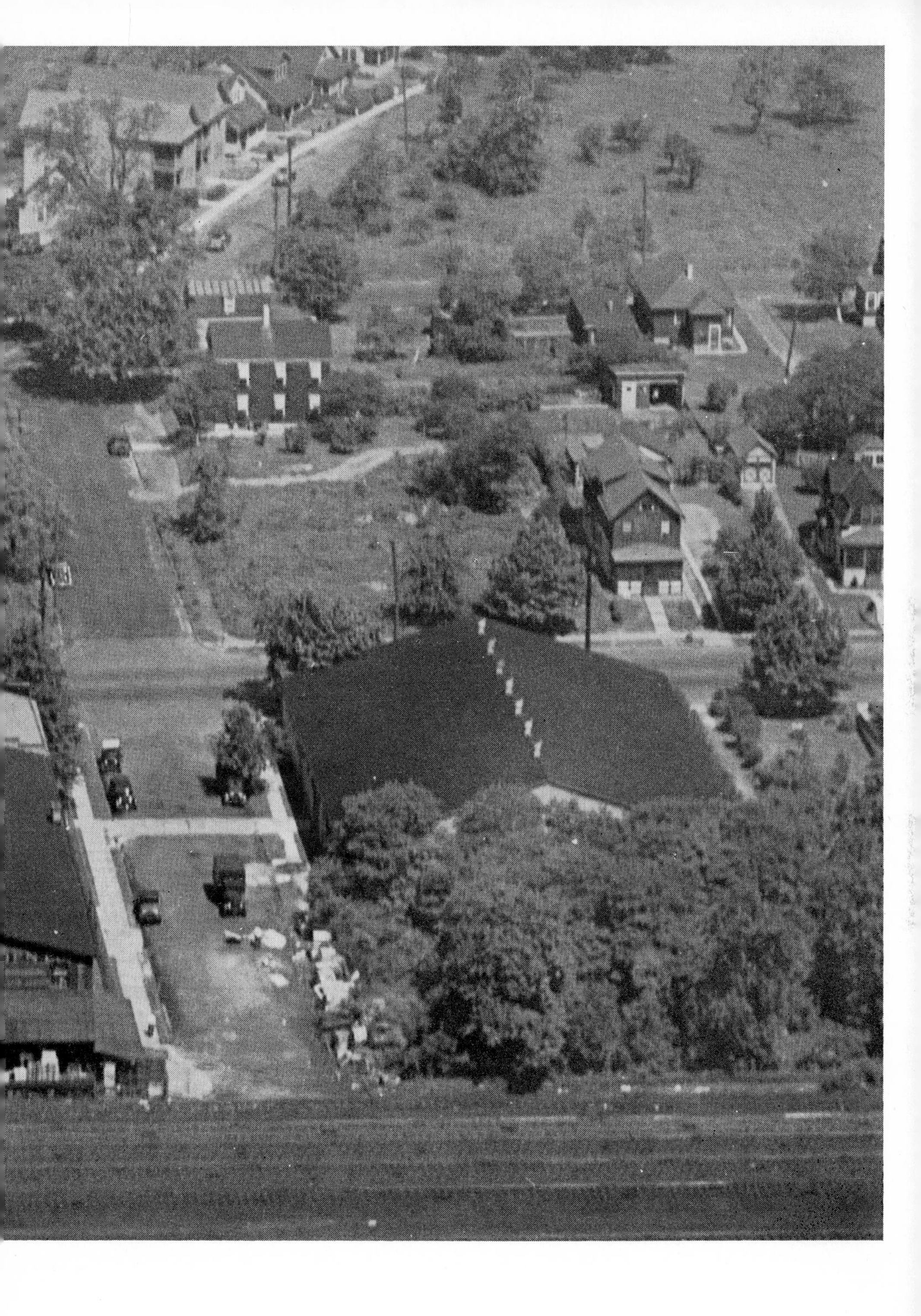

An aerial view of the Quinn & Boden plant in 1933.

Looking out of a plane window today, fifty years later, one envisions very little that resembles the 1906 establishment.

The Cue-Bee Club, for the employees, erected in 1936 to the memory of M. F. Quinn.

Readers at work in the proofroom. Soundproofed walls completely eliminate noise from adjoining rooms.

A battery of linotype machines begin the process of manufacturing a book.

Monotype keyboards, another method used in composing type. These machines perforate the paper spools used on the casting machines.

Monotype casting machines. The second unit used in the monotype operation. Here the individual characters are cast and collated as galleys of type.

A floorman breaking up type into the correct page size. This is known as "make-up."

A portion of the foundry, showing the operation of a molding press.

A general view of the pressroom.

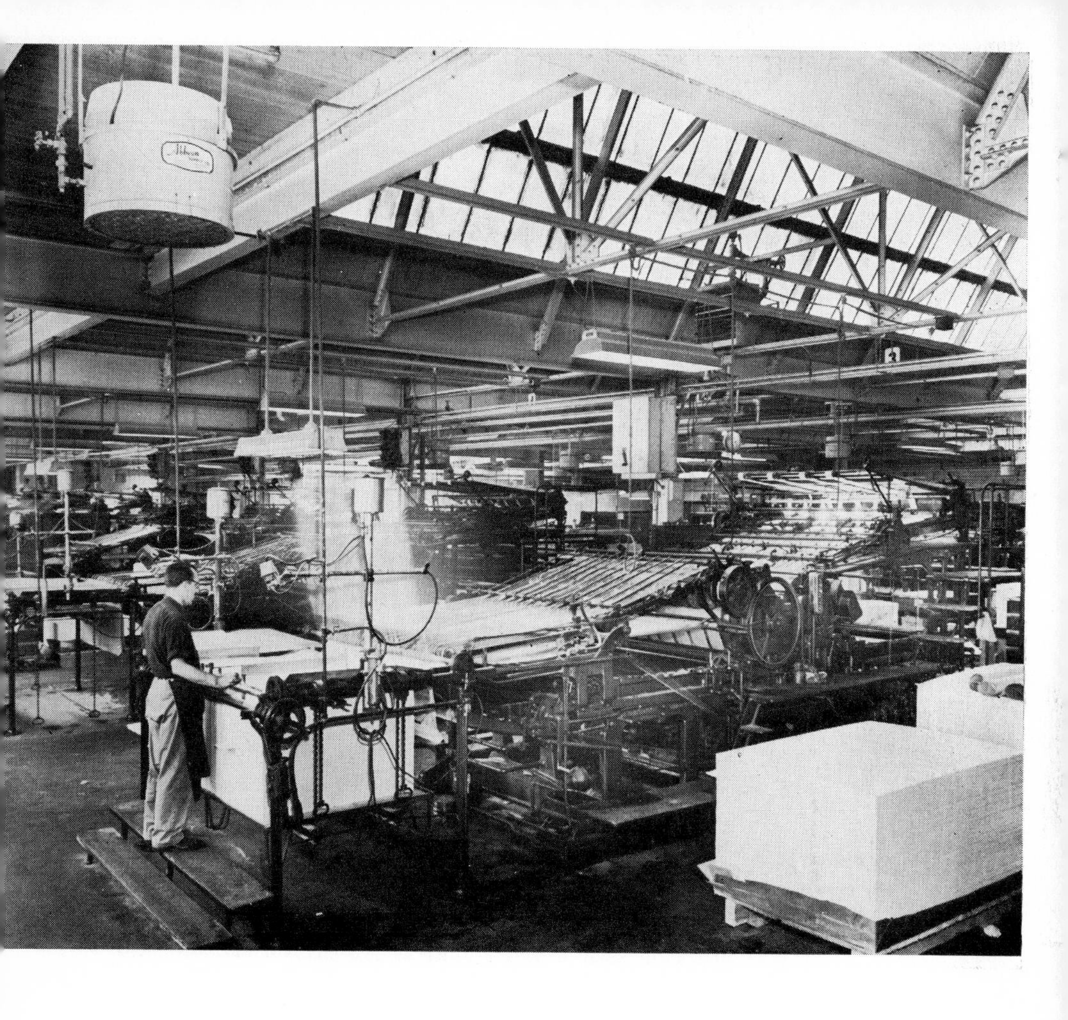

A pressman stands at the delivery end of the press watching for color variation and other imperfections.

Skids of printed sheets are transferred from the pressroom to the folding department where they are folded into "signatures."

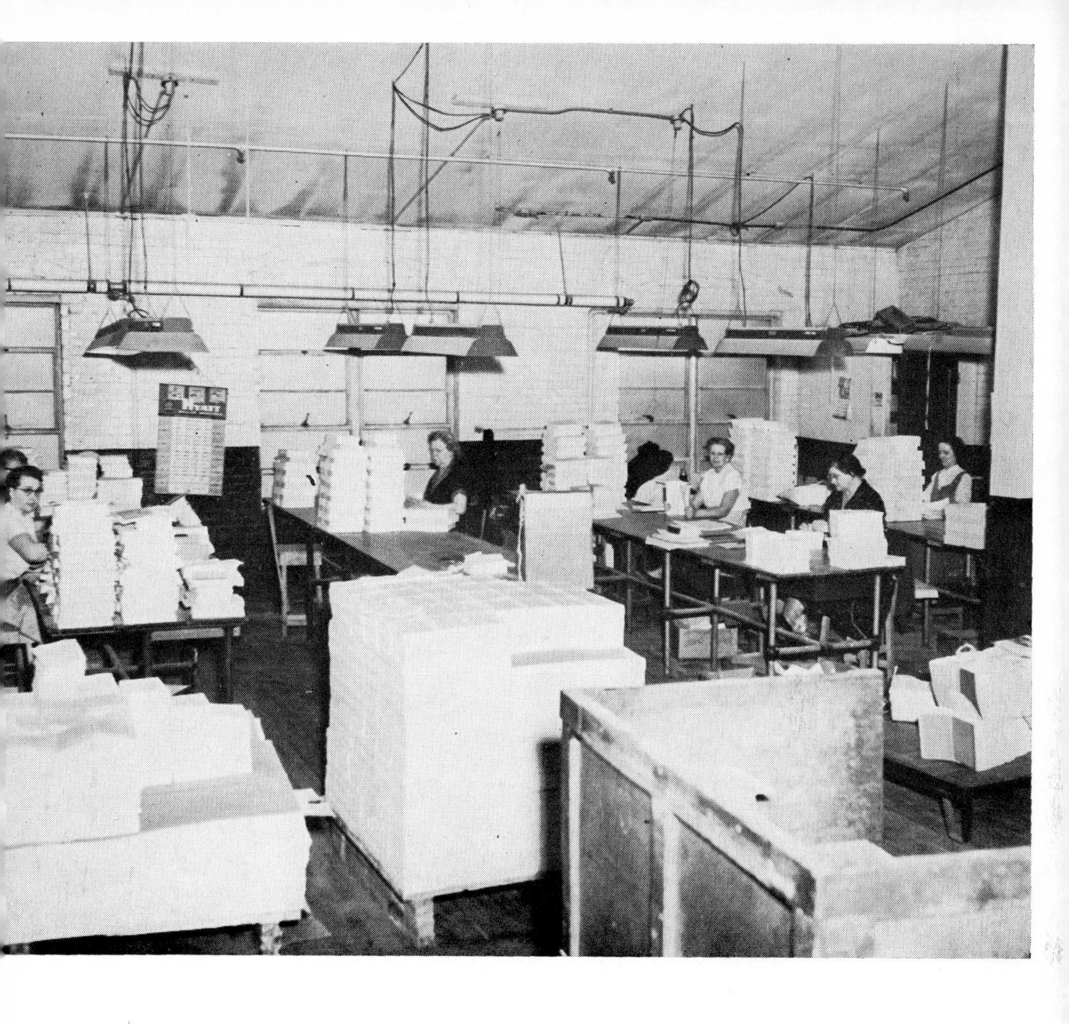

The pasting department. Here all necessary handwork is done on the signatures before they are "gathered."

Signatures are collated into their proper sequence on a gathering machine.

A battery of sewing machines, showing part of the conveyor belt system.

The books are then compressed, or nipped, and given an application of glue.

The tumbler cutter is a high-speed machine which trims three sides of the book to a predetermined size.

On this rounder and backer (foreground) *the book is given the traditional round back then, moving on a conveyor to the lining-up machine* (background), *the necessary reinforcement is applied to the back to hold the book in its cover.*

Covers are made on a casemaking machine from a continuous web of cloth.

A stamping press, where the book title, author and publisher's names are impressed on the cover in either foil or real gold.

When ink instead of foil or gold is used, this type of stamping press performs the operation.

The final step in the assembly is the casing-in machine, where the cover is permanently applied to the book.

An inspection line, where books are examined, wrapped, and delivered into an automatic carton-sealing machine.

The book is completed. Partial view of loading dock, where trucks are loaded with books for delivery.